HELLCATS

The 12th Armored Division in World War II

September 15, 1942 to December 17, 1945

Library of Congress Cataloging-in-Publication Data

Ferguson, John C. (John Craig), 1959-
     Hellcats: the 12th Armored Division in World War II,
     September 15, 1942 to December 17, 1945 / John C. Ferguson.--
     1st ed.
     p. cm.
     Includes bibliographical references and index.
     ISBN 1-880510-88-X (pbk.)
    1. United States. Army. Armored Division, 12th--History. 2. World
War, 1939-1945--Regimental histories--United States. 3. World War,
1939-1945--Campaigns--Western Front. I. Title.

D769.305312th .F47 2004
940.54'1273--dc22

                                   2004015112

State House Press
McMurry University, Box 637
Abilene, Texas 79697
(325) 793-4682
www.mcwhiney.org

Printed in the United States of America

1-880510-88-X
10 9 8 7 6 5 4 3 2 1

Book Designed by Rosenbohm Graphic Design

HELLCATS

The 12th Armored Division in World War II

JOHN C. FERGUSON

State ✦ House
Press
McMurry University
Abilene, Texas

CONTENTS

All photos are from the 12th Armored Division Memorial Museum historical collection.

PREFACE

It is with great pleasure that I am writing the preface to the history of the Hellcats. I was elated when John Ferguson introduced me to the idea of putting this book together for everyone to have access to the information.

The 12th Armored Association and Museum in historic downtown Abilene, Texas, mean more to my family and me than I can ever put into words. My father, PFC Tom T. Wilmeth, was killed in action on April 22, 1945. We never knew the real story of what happened to my father until I was led via the Internet to Dr. Vernon Williams in Abilene. This very busy man took the time to sit down with me and begin my search for information. Many heartfelt thanks to Dr. Williams. Here I was a sixty-one-year-old war orphan finally learning what happened to my father, one of the greatest loves of my life.

Through Dr. Williams I found the 12th Armored Association and the surviving Hellcats—what a thrill! These men are so special. They don't tell you of the hardships they went through at war. They don't tell you of the final winter of the war being the coldest ever on record and how they were so poorly clothed and nearly froze to death. They don't tell you what it was like in a freezing foxhole with a hot meal only at random times. Most of them survived near death situations and brought home wounds to deal with for the rest of their lives. The wounds the Hellcats brought home were physical and emotional. Thank God they have begun to tell their stories.

The veterans who tell us their experiences tell the real story of how it was. We can read all the books about World War II, but the men who came home are the ones who were there and lived through the hell of war. The amazing thing about the Hellcats is that instead of telling about the grueling times they lived through, they smile, laugh, and tell of the hilarity of all the funny stories and situations. They are full of humility and shrug their shoulders saying, "Oh, I just did what I needed to do," or "Oh, I was just a kid and decided I'd join up." The Hellcats flew the banner saying *Delinda Est Mal*—Latin for "Evil Must Be Destroyed"—and they lived every word of it.

World War II was a united effort by our whole country. Everyone in the United States sacrificed something in some way, not to mention the far-reaching losses that broke many, many hearts. Speaking as a World War II orphan, I can tell you that the trauma of the loss never really goes away. It affects children more than any adult can ever realize. We are so proud of our father, Tom T., who made the ultimate sacrifice for the love of his family and his country. We are also grateful to all the others who made this same sacrifice and to those in the Armed Forces today. People are forgetting about World War II and that is sad. After all, history repeats itself and we have to look back to see where we are going.

I especially want to thank George Hatt, a very special surviving Hellcat, who has taken not only me but also my mother, Martha Wilmeth Lyle; my brother, Thomas L. Wilmeth; and my sister, Donna Wilmeth McLaren, into his heart. He is a kind, loving gentleman who cares. George also has a wonderful, loving family who has embraced us as well.

Hellcats, yes, they are my heroes! I toss many bouquets and accolades their way. They were the "Mystery Men" and should not be forgotten. We will never be able to thank them enough for all they did to keep our country a free nation.

Karolyn Wilmeth Hendrix
Daughter of Tom T. Wilmeth

FOREWORD

It would be impossible to tell the full story of the deeds and heroism of men of the 12th Armored Division during their five months of unflagging combat against the Germans. Every officer and enlisted man in the division performed heroically in forming a combat team feared by our enemies and respected by our allies.

Many of our comrades were left along the way, from the Maginot Line to Austria. To the memory of those who gave their lives that the enemy in Europe might be defeated, let us dedicate these pages. May those gallant dead live here as they will live forever in the hearts of those who fought beside them.

We know not what we shall be called upon to do in the future, but we do know that, whatever our mission may be, it will be accomplished with the same magnificent fighting spirit which has given this division a record of achievement equaled by few. Nothing can stop us; little can delay us.

Roderick R. Allen
Major General, Commanding
Written for *A History of the United States 12th Armored Division*, published in 1946

This book is respectfully dedicated to the many soldiers of the 12th Armored Division who did not survive to reunite with their friends and families. These are the men who purchased with their lives the freedom that our nation enjoys today. Wherever there is a fallen American soldier, there is a seed of the tree of liberty.

This publication was made possible in part by
the family of Karolyn Wilmeth Hendrix
in loving memory of their father
PFC Tom T. Wilmeth
17th Armored Infantry Battalion, Company B
Killed in action April 22, 1945

INTRODUCTION

Shortly after the conclusion of the First World War in 1918, the United States of America voluntarily surrendered its position of military supremacy that had made possible the Allied victory over Germany and her cohorts. During the post-war disillusionment of the twenties and the worldwide economic depression of the thirties, America's military might shrank almost to insignificance. The great United States Army that had filled Frenchmen with hope and Germans with despair in 1917 became little more than a hollow shell.

While many people in America clung to their isolationist tendencies, others grew alarmed at the brutality of the Japanese in China and other Pacific Ocean areas, as well as the naked aggression of Germany in Europe. As the Imperial Japanese Army plundered Nanking and occupied French Indo-China, and the German Nazi Army brutally attacked and overran Poland, Denmark, the Netherlands, Belgium, and France, the United States finally gave serious attention to the dilapidated state of its armed forces. In late 1939 the United States Army, including the National Guard and the Army Air Corps, numbered approximately 400,000 soldiers. Of that number only 188,565 soldiers were on active duty, and that reduced figure included the Philippine Scouts. These numbers are unimpressive indeed when compared to those of Germany and Japan, the two most aggressive powers of the time. The Imperial Japanese Army and the trained reserve of Japan totaled 6,750,000 in 1939. In that same year the German active and reserve army and air forces included 4,129,000 troops. In 1940 this figure was raised to over 6,000,000.[1]

During the course of the national emergency and the subsequent war, or the years of 1939 to 1945, the United States Army increased in size dramatically. By August 1940 the Army had expanded from a total of six divisions to eight infantry divisions, one cavalry division, and one armored division, all of which were under strength. Active mobilization of the Army began in September 1940 when President Roosevelt began calling the National Guard divisions into federal service, and Congress passed the Selective Service Act. By the time Japan attacked the United States at Pearl Harbor, some thirty-six divisions had been organized.[2] During the war the United States mobilized ninety-two divisions and maintained eighty-nine. The Philippine Division was destroyed in combat, and the Army deactivated two divisions.[3] During the course of the war the size of the armored force of the United States grew from one armored division in August 1940 to sixteen armored divisions in December 1943. Those sixteen armored divisions were maintained until the end of the war.[4]

This is the story of one of those sixteen armored divisions.

"The defeat of Germany was quickened by the speed of the American armor."

Field Marshal Gerd Von Rundstedt
German Commander, 1945

CHAPTER 1

Creation of the 12th Armored Division

In September 1940 the United States Army began inducting National Guard divisions from the states into national service to quickly increase the size of the Army. But the National Guard of 1940 consisted of only eighteen divisions, and America's war planners believed that a much larger Army was necessary to engage in any type of offensive action overseas in either Europe or Asia, or certainly both. So new divisions had to be created.[5]

Most of the new divisions created by the Army were infantry divisions, as it is the infantry soldier who has historically fought and won battles and wars. But it was evident to observers that the shockingly sudden collapse of France in May 1940 was brought about largely as a result of German armor. The impact of massive formations of tanks on the battlefield was unmistakable, and the United States Army determined to have sufficient numbers of armored units.[6]

The basic component of the armored force was the armored division. The division was designed to be a self-sufficient combined arms team capable of sustained independent action. An armored division was made up of tanks, field artillery, infantry, and all the necessary support units. As designed by the War Department in 1940, an armored division would consist of 12,697 officers and enlist-

Chief of Staff Colonel John L. Ryan, Jr., confers with officers while planning the construction of Camp Campbell, Kentucky.

ed men. Armored divisions had a great volume of firepower from the tanks and artillery, and could move very rapidly as a result of being mechanized, or having the infantry carried to the scene of battle in vehicles.[7]

The 12th Armored Division was one of thirty-eight divisions, including nine armored divisions, activated in 1942. In the spring of that year Lieutenant General Leslie J. McNair, Commanding General of the Army Ground Forces, selected the senior officers of the proposed new division.[8]

General McNair's choices for the 12th Armored Division included the following:

- Commander—Brigadier General Carlos Brewer
- Assistant Commander—
  Brigadier General Thomas J. Camp
- Artillery Commander—Colonel Bernard F. Luebbermann
- G-1 (Administration)—Major Hugh Mair
- G-2 (Intelligence)—Lieutenant Colonel Neil S. Edmond
- G-3 (Operations and Training)—
  Lieutenant Colonel Richard B. Evans
- G-4 (Supply and Logistics)—
  Lieutenant Colonel Charles F. Howard[9]

After being selected, General Brewer, General Camp, and Colonel Luebbermann went to the headquarters of the Army Ground Forces for a week of orientation. Then on July 6, 1942 General Brewer began a month of special instruction at the Command and General Staff School at Fort Leavenworth, Kansas. His general staff, or the officers designated G-1 through G-4, joined him at Fort Leavenworth. While these officers attended the Command and General Staff School, the assistant division commander attended a special course at the Infantry School, and the division artillery commander attended a special course at the Field Artillery School. Other key officers of the proposed division attended intensive courses at their respective branch or service schools at the same time.[10]

Major General Carlos Brewer, division commander, speaks with a tanker at Camp Campbell.

As was the case with other divisions, the 12th Armored Division was formed around a "cadre," a trained core of officers and enlisted soldiers from another division. The parent unit for the 12th was the 8th Armored Division, and most of the men of the 8th had originally come from the 2nd Cavalry Division. The 2nd Cavalry Division, based at Fort Riley Kansas, was one of the last holdouts of the old horse-cavalry days and was inactivated on July 15, 1942.[11]

When the War Department decided to break up the 2nd Cavalry Division in June 1942, many of the men went to Fort Knox where they joined the

Colonel Ryan reading the order that activated the 12th Armored Division at Camp Campbell, Kentucky, on September 15, 1942.

General Brewer salutes the colors as the new division passes in review, September 15, 1942.

New recruits and transfers from other units arrive at Camp Campbell to fill out the ranks of the 12th Armored Division.

newly created 8th Armored Division. At Fort Knox the cavalrymen were reclassified, with most of the men going to the infantry. After reclassification many of the men were promoted to sergeant, and after little more than a month in the 8th Armored Division, great numbers of the former cavalrymen shipped out to Camp Campbell where they became the cadre for the new 12th Armored Division. The entire cadre of the infantry regiment came from the old 2nd Cavalry Division, although cadres for other units came from other sources.

Each of the infantry companies had an initial cadre of twenty-five men, which included the company first sergeant, supply sergeant, platoon sergeants, and squad leaders. These were the men who were to train the mass influx of new recruits that made up the bulk of the division.[12]

The not-yet-activated 12th Armored Division would be created at Camp Campbell, a newly constructed Army post straddling the Kentucky-Tennessee line. Newly promoted Major General Brewer and his staff arrived there on August 8, 1942, to begin laying the groundwork for the division. By the middle of August the remainder of the cadre of 216 officers and 1,460 enlisted men had arrived at Camp Campbell. These men stayed busy drawing up training schedules, designing obstacle courses, receiving training equipment, and preparing to receive the thousands of new men about to join the unit. During the next week the remainder of the officer complement, some 450 officers, arrived at Camp Campbell. These officers came from service schools, officer candidate schools, and the officer replacement pool.[13]

An early highlight of the division-to-be was the first

Tankers prepare their Browning 30-caliber machineguns for inspection.

Portable kitchens such as this often accompanied the soldiers when training in the field.

Negotiating the obstacle course became a part of the daily routine.

Physical training was a never-ending activity.

formal guard mount on August 17. Preliminary planning continued, with extra classes at night for the officers, until the activation day finally arrived. In a formal ceremony attended by military and civilian dignitaries, Chief of Staff Colonel John L. Ryan, Jr. read the order activating the division, and Major General Carlos Brewer officially assumed command of the 12th Armored Division. General Brewer received the division colors, then he in turn presented colors to each of the subordinate unit commanders.[14]

The initial organization of the division consisted of the following elements:

- Headquarters, 12th Armored Division
- Headquarters Company, 12th Armored Division
- 43rd Armored Regiment (3 battalions)
- 44th Armored Regiment (3 battalions)
- 56th Armored Infantry Regiment (3 battalions)
- 92nd Armored Reconnaissance Battalion
- 119th Armored Engineer Battalion (4 companies plus a bridge company)
- 493rd Armored Field Artillery Battalion (3 batteries, 6 howitzers each)
- 494th Armored Field Artillery Battalion (3 batteries, 6 howitzers each)
- 495th Armored Field Artillery Battalion (3 batteries, 6 howitzers each)
- 82nd Armored Medical Battalion
- Supply Battalion, 12th Armored Division

- Headquarters, 12th Armored Division Trains
  (included maintenance battalion)
- Headquarters Company, 12th Armored Division Trains
- 152nd Armored Signal Company
- Service Company, 12th Armored Division[15]

After Division Chaplain Lieutenant Colonel Silas Decker blessed the flags of each of the units, General Brewer addressed the assemblage, concluding with these remarks.

"We are a new division, but with a great heritage. The Armored Force is recognized as the elite branch of our ground forces. We are the vanguard, or shock troops, in battle. Men of the Armored Force have been outstanding in their soldierly qualities wherever they have come in contact with other troops. They are neater, more courteous, better trained, and justly proud of their unit. We have everything to develop a top combat division here at Camp Campbell. We have a splendid camp and training facilities, good climate, friendly communities, and most important of all, outstanding leaders in our commissioned officers and enlisted cadre. I am sure that you will not be satisfied any more than I will until the 12th Armored Division has proved its worth and is recognized as one of the best in the Army. To our country we pledge our lives and our honor, and we promise victory."[16]

The initial organization of the division called for a strength of 14,620 men, with 4,848 men in the two armored regiments, 2,389 soldiers in the infantry regiment, and 2,127 men in the artillery battalions.[17]

Filler replacements, which made up the bulk of the enlisted ranks, began arriving on October 24. Most of these men came from reception centers, and had been in the Army for only a few days. As the new men arrived in large groups at Camp Campbell, host units, comprised of staff from the infantry regiment, met the recruits and guided their initial activities. The host units took the new recruits to their regimental areas where they received hot meals, showers, and bunk assignments. Over the next several days the men were interviewed as to their job qualifications, filled out numerous forms, had physical examinations, were classified or assigned jobs, and were

Lieutenant General Jacob L. Devers, commander of all U.S. armored forces, inspects the 12th Armored Division at Camp Campbell. General Devers later became commander of the Sixth Army Group, under which the 12th served in France and Germany.

sent to units. Physical training and lectures filled much of the early days of the new recruits.

Formal training for the division began on November 10, 1942 with the implementation of the Mobilization Training Program. This program outlined a detailed thirty-five week training schedule for the division that included thirteen weeks of individual or basic training, eleven weeks of unit training, and eleven weeks of combined training.[18]

The initial phase of training consisted of instruction in the fundamentals of military life to include military courtesy, discipline, sanitation, first aid, and drill. Each of the men had to learn the basic skills of a soldier before he could become a specialist. Training of the men included great emphasis on physical conditioning and sports. In addition to helping the men stay in shape, sports taught the men how to function as a team.[19]

The second period of instruction consisted of training the men in units, from the squad to the regiment. Training in this phase emphasized field exercises and living in the field for days at a time. During unit training the soldiers learned tactical procedures of larger units, and how to maneuver and act as units rather than as individuals. Engineers learned how to build field fortifications and bridges, and

Engineers building a pontoon bridge across the Cumberland River.

lay minefields. Medics learned such skills as how to evacuate wounded while under fire and how to move wounded across streams.

The final phase of instruction consisted of eleven weeks of combined-arms training to merge the different types of units into a cohesive whole. Infantry, tanks, and artillery learned to work and fight together through a series of large-scale exercises. Day and night operations, lasting several days, culminated in maneuvering one division against another, in wooded as well as open terrain.[20]

> We were new to armored but had good military service under our belts. Camp Campbell was new; in fact they were still building barracks when we arrived. After building so-called duck boards for sidewalks to keep out the mud, we all, including our new officers, unpacked and washed dishes, set up beds, and started learning to be armored.
>
> Tech Sergeant Robert Grebl
> B Company, 66th Armored
> Infantry Battalion

While the division trained at Camp Campbell, General Brewer held a contest to come up with a suitable nickname for the division. Private Francis Beckman (Menco, Kansas) of the 493rd Armored Field Artillery Battalion submitted the winning entry, with the nickname "Hellcats," which General Brewer formally adopted on February 1, 1943. Private Beckman's reward for coming up with the name was a three-day pass. Another diversion from the arduous training schedule occurred on April 1, 1943, when the 56th Armored Infantry Regiment received orders to provide protection to President Roosevelt while he was on a train trip through Tennessee.

General Brewer's headquarters during the Tennessee Maneuvers.

Portable chow hall set up in the field during the Tennessee Maneuvers.

The soldiers guarded the railroad line from Tullahoma, Tennessee to the Mississippi River.[21]

After the division successfully completed the proscribed Mobilization Training Program, the Hellcats continued with tactical and conditioning exercises. Endless road marches, both on foot and in vehicles, carried the men of the 12th over a wide stretch of the states of Kentucky and Tennessee. Training continued through the spring and summer of 1943, as the division prepared for the upcoming Tennessee Maneuvers, which would pit multiple divisions against each other. One of the highlights of the training was a five-day river crossing exercise staged on the Cumberland River. This was followed by intensive air-ground training back on the Camp Campbell reservations. Many of the men grumbled that combat couldn't be a tough as these extended field exercises![22]

In preparation for the upcoming Second Army Number Three Tennessee Maneuvers, the men of the Hellcat Division completely packed up their personal and military belongings, and prepared to leave Camp Campbell, which had been their home for more than a year. The men knew that at the conclusion of the maneuvers they would not return to Campbell, as their barracks and battalion areas had already been taken over by a new infantry division. On September 3, 1943, long columns of military vehicles began to depart from Camp Campbell and head south toward the Tennessee Maneuver Area. There the "Red" army would oppose the "Blue" army, with each army consisting of one armored and two infantry

Hellcats with all their belongings ready to move out at the end of the Tennessee Manuevers.

divisions. Tanks, half-tracks, self-propelled artillery, jeeps, trucks, and command cars filled the roads as the division moved in convoy to the new division command post near Lebanon, Tennessee.[23]

The Tennessee Maneuvers lasted from September 6 through the first week of November, and consisted of a series of nine operations or problems. The 12th, designated the "Blue" armored division, began the exercise with an air-ground demonstration, showing how fighter-bombers and troops on the ground can work effectively together. The Hellcats then went on the offensive, conducting a night march followed by a daylight attack on the rear of a Red division. Utilizing the speed and mobility of the armored division, the Hellcats captured large numbers of opposing infantry.[24]

The Second Army Maneuvers continued for weeks, during which all the units involved learned how to move massive numbers of men and vehicles from place to place, using limited roads. Problems of reconnaissance and supply had to be overcome, and new innovations experimented with, such as using parachute drops to provide necessities to cut-off units. In mock battles the division attacked and captured enemy-held bridges, defended bridges from enemy attack, and crossed rivers without bridges.[25]

Realistic operations were carried out during night and day, in the most difficult conditions of weather and terrain. Weaknesses were discovered and many lessons were learned.

Another benefit of the maneuvers was to show who the natural leaders were, which leaders could think and act under pressure and fatigue, and which ones could not. At the conclusion of the maneuvers, Lieutenant General Fredendall, the Second Army Commander, stated that the 12th Armored Division was the first one since he had been Army commander to be employed correctly throughout the maneuvers, and that it set a new standard of performance for such divisions.[26]

The Hellcats benefited greatly from the extended field exercise and emerged from the maneuvers a tougher, smarter, more experienced outfit. At the conclusion of the Tennessee Maneuvers the 12th Armored Division headed west—to Texas.

*"It is our hope that many of you at the end
of your training period will decide to remain in
Abilene, but if you return to your homes,
we trust you will carry back with you many happy
memories of the days spent in Camp Barkeley
and in the city of Abilene."*

W. W. Hair, Mayor of Abilene, March 28, 1941

CHAPTER 2

Abilene and Camp Barkeley

In 1880 the Texas and Pacific Railway Company pushed westward from Fort Worth, busily extending its railroad track across the arid expanses of West Texas in an effort to build a transcontinental railroad across the southern portion of the United States. As the track-laying crews approached Taylor County, a group of landowners and speculators met with representatives from the Texas and Pacific Company to discuss the creation of a new community adjacent to the railroad. John Simpson, owner of the Hashknife Ranch on Cedar Creek in northern Taylor County, hosted a meeting that included S.L. Chalk, John T. Berry, and the enterprising brothers John and Claiborne W. Merchant from nearby Callahan County. In their discussions with officials from the railroad, the group decided that a town would be established in the northeast corner of Taylor County, approximately 150 miles west of Fort Worth.

The site chosen for the new town lay between Cedar and Big Elm creeks, on and adjacent to the Hashknife Ranch. C.W. Merchant named the town after Abilene, Kansas, in the hopes that the new community would become a great cattle-shipping center, as its

Aerial view of Abilene, circa 1940.

namesake had become. T&P employees laid out the streets and staked off the lots for the town even before the railroad reached the area. The first train pulled into Abilene on February 27, 1881, and on that same day local Presbyterians established the first church, in a tent. On the cold and clear morning of March 15, 1881, the town fathers held an auction to sell town lots, and during the course of the auction hopeful citizens purchased more than 170 lots. The new community of Abilene, Texas, was off to a promising beginning.[27]

The founders of Abilene created the town to serve the agricultural industry of the area, and Abilene remained a farming and ranching community for many years. Abilene did indeed become a center for shipping cattle, as well as horses and wool. Other agricultural products, primarily livestock related, also went out from Abilene. A regional farm and ranch center, Abilene also became home to all the businesses a community needs and desires. Wholesale grocers, banks, hotels, and retail stores all became established businesses in Abilene.

Scholastic opportunities did not go lacking in the West Texas town, as higher education soon came to Abilene. In 1892 classes began at the Abilene Baptist College, founded by a coalition of

A view of the site of Camp Barkeley on the prairie of southern Taylor County, Texas. The hills in the distance are over four miles from where the photo was taken.

Baptists and Abilene businessmen. The Church of Christ followed by establishing a school in 1906, and in 1923 the Methodists opened McMurry College.[28] These schools eventually became known as Hardin-Simmons University, Abilene Christian University, and McMurry University.

Over the years Abilene grew slowly but steadily, and by 1940 the community was home to some 26,000 inhabitants.[29] While many types of businesses existed in Abilene, the economy of the area was still largely based on agriculture and the newly developing oil industry, both of which were adversely affected during the Great Depression of the 1930s. Like many other communities and small cities, Abilene was still struggling to recover from the Depression by 1940. With the world in crisis, and wars raging in Europe and Asia, one way to assist the economic recovery of Abilene would be to have a training camp for the growing American military force.

The Abilene area of West Texas has a long and proud military history dating back to 1851 when the Army established a post to protect the settlers along the edge of civilization in West Texas. Fort Phantom Hill, fifteen miles north of present-day Abilene, was the northernmost of a line of Army camps that extended from the Rio Grande upward into the high rolling plains of Texas. The Army abandoned Fort Phantom Hill after only a few years, but the military heritage of West Texas was begun.[30]

*Camp Barkeley
Abilene, Texas
9:40 am.   2-6-'41
Sewer Disposal plant*

The multi-million dollar contract to build Camp Barkeley employed thousands of civilian laborers.

Prior to World War I, Abilene had established a local National Guard organization. When President Woodrow Wilson called all the National Guard units into national service, the guardsmen from Texas and Oklahoma combined to form the 36th Division. The Abilene National Guard detachment became part of the 142nd Infantry Regiment of the 36th Division. After training at Camp Bowie in Fort Worth, the 36th Division sailed in 1918 to France, where the men served honorably and well in the First World War.[31]

With the sudden collapse of France and its surrender to Nazi Germany in the summer of 1940, America began to seriously consider its defensive preparedness. As military spending nationwide increased, members of the Abilene Chamber of Commerce began to actively petition the War Department in an effort to have the Army build a training base in Abilene. When a hoped-for Army Air Corps pilot training base went to nearby San Angelo, city fathers renewed their efforts to have an Army base built in Abilene.[32]

Attorney Bob Wagstaff, Chamber of Commerce President and oil distributor W.P. "Dub" Wright, publisher Bernard Hanks, merchant

Initially all of the soldiers at Camp Barkeley lived in tents that had wooden floors and partial walls. These are the frames for the tents.

Ernest Grissom, and banker Malcom Meek formed a military committee to convince the Army that it should build a facility in Abilene. Under the leadership of these men, the City of Abilene secured and offered to the War Department a cantonment or camp area of some two thousand acres, with an additional maneuver area of more than sixty thousand acres. The city would purchase this land, located approximately seven miles south of Abilene, and lease it to the government for the sum of one dollar per year.

The proposal was too good for the Army to pass up, and late in November 1940 the War Department announced it would accept the Abilene offer if the city could raise the money to purchase the land. Malcolm Meek, president of the Citizens National Bank, headed a fund-drive effort that raised the money in one week.[33]

Construction of the camp began as soon as the government signed the contract with the City of Abilene. The work began during the first week of January 1941, and by the end of that week, 2,600 men were employed at the camp. By the end of the month the labor

Station No. 2
Date: 2-27-41

Camp Barkeley.
Abilene, Texas
1:22 pm   2-27-'41
Station 2

Canvas-covered, wooden framed tents served as barracks for the men at Barkeley. Later, two of the tent frames were pushed together and covered with plywood to provide a slightly less unpleasant housing. The new structures were called "hutments."

force consisted of 7,000 men, endeavoring to complete the camp as quickly as possible. Rainy weather slowed the progress, as the site of the Army camp became a sea of mud.[34]

The Army Corps of Engineers drew up the plan for the new camp, with the intention that it would be a temporary facility, used only for the duration of the war. Most of the men, officers as well as enlisted soldiers, initially lived in tents with wooden floors. The tents had sides framed in with two-by-four lumber, thirty inches high, covered with wire screen. That way the sides of the tents could be rolled up for air circulation in nice weather, while keeping the mosquitoes and flies out.[35]

On January 10, 1941, the War Department announced that the base in Abilene would be called Camp Barkeley, honoring the memory of a World War I soldier. David Bennes Barkley, from Laredo,

David Barkley

Texas has always had her share of brave young men willing to serve their country. One that should not be forgotten is Medal of Honor recipient David Barkley.

Born in 1899 to Josef and Antonia Cantu Barkley in Laredo, Texas, young Barkley joined the Army in August 1917. That he chose to enlist in the Army is not surprising, since his father was a career soldier, rising to the rank of master sergeant with nearly thirty years of service.

David Barkley trained at Camp Travis at San Antonio before being assigned to the 36th Division at Camp Bowie in Fort Worth. After the 36th Division went to France, Barkley was transferred to Company A, 356th Infantry Regiment, 89th Division. During the closing days of the First World
War, Private Barkley and another soldier volunteered to swim across the Meuse River near Pouilly to gain information about the strength and location of the German enemy. The two men successfully crossed the river, despite a hail of enemy bullets. After reconnoitering the enemy positions and drawing a map of their locations, Barkley and his companion reentered the water, returning to U.S. lines with the desired information. But before he could reach the American side of the river, young Barkley drowned. He died on November 9, 1918, only two days before the end of the war.

For his exceptional courage David Barkley received the Medal of Honor, our country's highest award for valor, as well as the French Croix de Guerre and the Italian Croce Merito. He was one of only three Texans to receive the Medal of Honor during World War I and was the first Hispanic from Texas to receive that decoration. His body lay in state at the Alamo, the only person other than Sam Houston to be so honored. David Barkley, a nineteen-year-old soldier from Texas, is an American hero.[37]

Texas, died while on an intelligence gathering mission behind enemy lines. For his exceptional courage the Army awarded him a posthumous Medal of Honor. The spelling of the new Army camp, with the extra "e," resulted from a clerical error that was never corrected.[36]

Soon after the Army named the base, Abilene residents learned that the inhabitants of Camp Barkeley would be their neighbors from north of the Red River—the 45th Division, Oklahoma National Guard. The first small contingent of Army troops arrived in Abilene on February 24, 1941, to help make the camp ready for the thousands of soldiers to follow. The bulk of the division arrived on

Aerial view of Camp Barkeley taken February 15, 1941. This was only 58 days after construction began.

February 28 as more than ten thousand soldiers passed down Pine Street on their way to Camp Barkeley.[38]

The 45th Division was a National Guard unit whose members came from New Mexico, Arizona, Colorado, and Oklahoma, with the majority of the men coming from the latter state. The 45th Division trained at Barkeley until the first of June, at which time the division went to nearby Camp Bowie, near Brownwood, to participate in the VIII Corps Texas Maneuvers. At the conclusion of the maneuvers the division returned to Abilene, training there until August, when the division moved to Louisiana.

The 45th Division returned to Camp Barkeley once more on October 4, 1941, and stayed until the middle of April 1942. During the latter stay at Camp Barkeley, the division was redesignated the 45th Infantry Division, to distinguish it from the growing number of armored divisions being created. The 45th Infantry Division departed Abilene for the last time in the middle of April 1942, going to the East Coast for additional training, before finally heading for North Africa and the invasion of Sicily in the summer of 1943.[39]

One of the 45th Division soldiers who later gained fame was the Pulitzer Prize-winning cartoonist Bill Mauldin. Born near

Alamogordo in southern New Mexico, Mauldin attended art school in Chicago, and was an accomplished cartoonist while still in his teens. Joining the National Guard in 1940, Private Mauldin came to Abilene as a rifleman in Company K, 180th Infantry Regiment. While in Abilene he married a young coed, who was a sophomore at Hardin-Simmons University, before he shipped out with the rest of his division in 1942.[40]

This building, across the street from the train depot, was the first United Service Organization (USO) recreation facility for soldiers in Abilene.

The 45th Division was not the only Army unit to utilize Camp Barkeley. In May 1941 the War Department announced that it would build a Medical Training Replacement Center at Barkeley. This school would train officers

This popular USO club was near the site of the present 12th Armored Division Museum on North 2nd Street in Abilene.

other than doctors to work primarily as administrators in the medical profession and in Army hospitals. In the spring of 1942, the Army expanded the medical training at Camp Barkeley to include an Officer Candidate School for the training of new officers who would go into the Medical Corps. During the course of the war, tens of thousands of medical personnel trained at Camp Barkeley, which became the Army's largest medical training facility.[41]

The next major military presence in Abilene was the 90th Division, first activated as a National Army division on August 25, 1917, during the First World War. At that time practically all of the junior officers came from Texas, and every one of the original complement of enlisted men came from either Texas or Oklahoma. The men chose as their insignia a monogram composed of the letters "T" and "O" superimposed. The division saw heavy combat in France

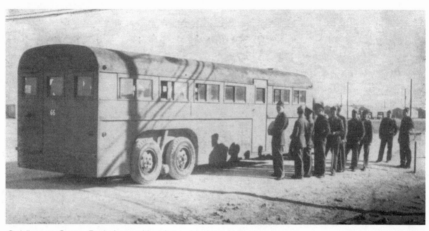

Soldiers at Camp Barkeley waiting for a ride into Abilene.

during the last months of World War I, and after brief occupation duty, it was deactivated in the summer of 1919.[42]

The 90th Division came back to life when the War Department activated it at Camp Barkeley on March 25, 1942. Redesignated as the 90th Infantry Division on May 20, 1942, the unit participated in the massive Third Army Number 1 Louisiana Maneuvers from January 28, 1943, until returning to Camp Barkeley on April 1. After more training in West Texas, the 90th Infantry Division departed Camp Barkeley for good in early September 1943.

> *The 45th Division marched down Pine Street and everybody was out on the curb to welcome them. You were just proud to be an American.*
> Cherry Gleason,
> Abilene resident

One regiment of the 90th Infantry Division assaulted Utah Beach on June 6, 1944, and the remainder of the division came ashore two days later. In heavy fighting in France and Germany, the "Tough 'Ombres," so nick-named because of the letters "T" and "O" on their shoulder patch, lost almost four thousand men killed in action or died of wounds, and an additional fourteen thousand wounded.[43]

Just as the 90th Infantry Division departed Camp Barkeley, the 11th Armored Division arrived from Camp Polk, Louisiana, with some units reaching Abilene as early as September 5. The tankers and armored infantry of the 11th barely had time to unpack and get settled in before moving on again. After being in West Texas only about seven weeks, the division departed for the Desert

Soldiers in uniform crowded the streets of Abilene from 1941 to 1945.

Training Center in California, arriving there the last week of October 1943.[44]

The massive influx of young men—20,000 arriving in the first month and up to 60,000 at Camp Barkeley's peak—was a blessing for Abilene, and most local inhabitants were genuinely happy to have the soldiers there. The young men spent a great amount of money in Abilene, and local firms conducted a great deal of business with the base. Abilene suppliers provided the camp with meat and vegetables for the numerous mess halls; milk, ice cream and other dairy products for consumption during meals as well as for off-duty snacks; and the always important soft drinks and the ice to cool them. Local oil companies provided gasoline and oil products for the Army, and local construction contractors continued to add new buildings at the base during the course of the war. Camp Barkeley had a huge positive economic impact on Abilene.

The young soldiers stationed at Camp Barkeley often had time off from their official duties, in the evenings or on weekends, and during those times the men flocked to Abilene and surrounding communities in search of entertainment. Many of the community leaders of Abilene had long viewed their home as a morally upright, some might say strict, community. A strong church and religious influence had kept Abilene "dry," continuing the legal prohibition of alcoholic beverages even after the national prohibition ended in

One of many parades through downtown Abilene during World War II.

1933. Some community leaders grew concerned at the thought of large numbers of healthy, physically active, energetic young soldiers coming to Abilene to seek rest and recreation, and possibly liquor or beer and female companionship.

To help fill the need for wholesome entertainment, a group of Abilene businessmen purchased the old Elks Lodge building downtown near the bus stop and gave the building to the Chamber of Commerce to be used as a recreation center for soldiers. The recreation hall opened in April 1941, and the Chamber of Commerce soon turned its operation over to the United Service Organization, or USO. The USO ultimately opened three additional clubs for the benefit of servicemen.

The USOs provided a place for the soldiers to unwind away from the strictures of military discipline. Professional staff as well as many volunteers greeted the soldiers and provided such things as books, magazines, soft drinks and sandwiches. Some of the USO clubs offered dance lessons, and local ladies formed an organization to provide dance partners for the soldiers. The Bluebonnet Brigade, formed in 1941, was an effort by local citizens to provide appropriately chaperoned young ladies to serve as dance partners and companions at the USO clubs.[45]

Churches, the Red Cross, and other organizations also provided recreational facilities for the soldiers, while many families pitched in and helped as well. The Army provided trucks or buses that brought the soldiers to a bus stop at the corner of Butternut and South 1st Streets, and many families would wait there to pick up soldiers they would adopt for a weekend. Over a short period of time, a warm and affectionate relationship grew between the people of Abilene and the soldiers at Camp Barkeley.

"Arriving at Camp Barkeley, we found a windy,
dusty place with plywood barracks.
As the hot Texas summer approached, we experi-
enced many long marches out into the limestone
hills and among the mesquite bushes."

Robert A. Stanton, Company A, 17th Armored Infantry Battalion

CHAPTER 3

The Hellcats Move to Texas

At the conclusion of the Tennessee Maneuvers, the Hellcat Division moved to Watertown, Tennessee, where it reorganized in accordance with War Department directives intended to make armored divisions more efficient fighting units with greater tactical flexibility. The War Department considered the previous organization of "heavy" armored divisions, with two armored regiments and one armored infantry regiment, somewhat cumbersome and unwieldy in combat, since the division was often split up into smaller task force units that combined tanks, infantry, and artillery. Experience in combat had shown that smaller units could be utilized more efficiently, so on September 15, 1943, the War Department issued a directive changing the organization of all armored divisions.[46]

The new "light" armored division organization replaced the previous two armored regiments (six battalions) with three tank battalions, but increased the size of the individual battalions. Each new battalion had three companies of medium tanks and one company of light tanks, plus six medium tanks mounting 105-millimeter howitzers, referred to as "assault guns."[47]

The armored infantry regiment was broken up into three separate battalions, but each battalion was increased in size from 700 men to

Lt. Aten of the 134th Ordnance Battalion and his wife at the Camp Barkeley Main Gate.

Soldier gets acquainted with an armadillo.

1,001 men, and a service company was added to each infantry battalion. Additionally, three combat command groups were instituted, these being Combat Command A, Combat Command B, and Combat Command R, or reserve. The theory was that the combat commands would be the tactical fighting units of the division, and each combat command would consist of a mix of tanks, artillery, and infantry, plus engineers, signal units, and any other required support units. The structure of the combat commands was not fixed, but flexible, depending upon the requirements of the mission at hand.[48]

In the 12th Armored Division, the 43rd and 44th Armored Regiments became the 43rd, 44th, 23rd, 714th, and 779th Tank Battalions. The new division organization called for only three tank battalions, so the 714th went to Fort Jackson, South Carolina, and the 779th went to Fort Knox, Kentucky. The 43rd, 44th, and 23rd remained with the Hellcat Division.

The 56th Armored Infantry Regiment became the 56th, 66th, and 17th Armored Infantry Battalions. The 92nd Armored Reconnaissance Battalion became the 92nd Cavalry Reconnaissance Squadron, Mechanized. The 119th Armored Engineer Battalion remained the same, but the Treadway Bridge Company was removed from the division.

Hellcats learning to use the bazooka anti-tank weapon.

The three field artillery battalions—the 493rd, 494th, and 495th— remained the same, as did the 82nd Armored Medical Battalion and the 152nd Armored Signal Company. The Supply Battalion was transferred intact to the Second Army, and the Division Service Company was disbanded, while the Maintenance Battalion was renamed the 134th Ordnance Maintenance Battalion. New additions to the division included a military police platoon and a division band.[49]

After the reorganization, the authorized strength of the division was 10,937 officers and enlisted men. Principal equipment included 186 medium tanks, 77 light tanks, 54 self-propelled 105-millimeter howitzers, and 501 halftrack armored personnel carriers.[50]

> It was a good location (for an Army camp), I thought, since the land was not suitable for anything else. The only green grass was found around the Headquarters building.
> Marvin Bertelson
> C Battery, 493rd Field Artillery

After the reorganization, the division turned its vehicles over to the new 14th Armored Division, then the men boarded trains at Watertown, Tennessee, on November 15 and headed south and west

Soldier shooting an M1 carbine from concealment.

to the rambling West Texas post of Camp Barkeley, near the city of Abilene. General Brewer and his staff arrived in Abilene on Wednesday, November 17, 1943, and the remainder of the division joined him by the following Saturday to occupy the quarters recently vacated by the 11th Armored Division.[51]

Not all the soldiers who came to Camp Barkeley and Abilene were enamored of the climate and natural geographic beauty of the area. West Texas is often windy, and there were very few trees to reduce the harsh effects of the stiff breezes. Many natives of the area contended that the winter of 1943-44 was an unusually wet one, and while the farmers and stock raisers welcomed the rain, the soldiers who had to train in the mud were not so receptive. Many soldiers complained of standing in mud up to their knees, with the wind blowing dust in their faces. Armadillos, rattlesnakes, skunks, mesquite trees, and prickly pear cactus were new species of fauna and flora to many of the soldiers, some of whom were not favorably impressed with the Texas plants and wildlife.

Married GIs had a tougher time in Abilene than the single men. The small farming and ranching community was not prepared for the sudden increase in population, and housing for married couples was in extremely short supply. One couple rented a seven foot by eleven foot room, with a sink, toilet, bed, and stove all in the same

Obstacle course at Camp Barkeley

room. Sometimes the young wives had to do housework for the homeowner, in addition to paying rent.[52]

The division quickly knuckled down to a tough training regimen, with formal classes and many field problems, or practical exercises. During their time at Camp Barkeley, each unit had training in its specific area of responsibility. Cooks learned how to prepare meals in the field and how to use the newly-developed dehydrated foods. Engineers exercised such practical skills as building roads, clearing mine fields, and constructing Bailey bridges from pre-fabricated steel components. Instruction for the infantry, tankers, and artillerymen became more realistic and imaginative, with emphasis placed on firing, maneuvering, and attacking. Physical conditioning continued to be stressed, with emphasis on team sports, and regular physical fitness testing. As the training at Camp Barkeley progressed, the units of the division spent at least one half of each month in the field, away from the Spartan comforts of the Camp Barkeley garrison. Many exercises, such as attacks on defensive positions, continued day and night for up to five days.

On February 11, 1944, the 44th Tank Battalion was detached from the 12th Armored Division, never again to rejoin the remainder of the unit. The 44th traveled by train to the West Coast, where it went aboard ships at the Portland, Oregon, Port of Embarkation on March 23, 1944. After leaving the United States, the 44th Tank Battalion first went to Australia, then to New Guinea and the Philippine Islands to fight the Japanese. Among other achievements, the 44th Tank

Infantrymen dismounting from a truck and charging into the hills of Camp Barkeley.

Battalion liberated the Santo Tomas American internment camp in Manila.[53]

The departure of the 44th left the division short one tank battalion, and during the last week of February 1944 the 714th Tank Battalion filled that vacancy. The 714th had been formed from the 3rd battalion of the old 44th Armored Regiment at the conclusion of the Tennessee Maneuvers, but had then been sent to Fort Jackson, South Carolina. Its assignment to the 12th Armored Division, then, was a type of homecoming for the men of the battalion.[54]

> *I had to use a laundromat. I would wait until 5 o'clock p.m. and then turn the hose on the car to cool it down so I could open the door. I'd do my wash and come home and hang them on the line. As I finished, the first ones would be dry.*
>
> Bulah Meyer, wife of Major Lawrence H. Meyer Headquarters, 12th Armored Division

An interesting feature of the artillery battalions that was perfected at Camp Barkeley was the use of small airplanes in conjunction with the artillery. Each artillery battalion had two Piper Cub airplanes, known in the Army as L-4s, with a pilot, observer, and ground crew for each plane. When accurate artillery fire was desired, the pilots flew the light aircraft over the targets, and observed the bursting of the artillery shells. Then the observer then would radio back to the ground crew any corrections needed to place the artillery shells on the target.

Soldiers on maneuvers at Camp Barkeley.

The L-4s seldom flew above 500 feet in altitude and could land on a runway as short as 150 to 200 feet in length. The air branch of the artillery service was known as the "grasshopper patrol" because they flew so close to the ground, hopping over trees, fences, and telephone lines. The ground-hugging technique was used to reduce the possibility of observation by enemy troops. The use of aircraft as artillery spotters was a great success and helped to account for the excellent accuracy of the artillery battalions.[55]

A unique organization within the 12th Armored Division was the 134th Ordnance Maintenance Battalion, known as the "Harvester Battalion." Before the beginning of World War II, the International Harvester Company of Chicago, Illinois, operated twenty-seven plants throughout the country, manufacturing trucks, tractors, and power generators. In early 1942 the Adjutant General of the Army authorized the Harvester Company to form a maintenance battalion from among its workers. Executives of the company were commissioned as officers in the Army and began recruiting from among their employees.

The Harvester Company used recruiting posters and circulars in its plants and dealerships, and within nine days after the start of the campaign 1,195 employees of the company applied for enlistment in

12th Armored Division soldiers and the Taylor County Sheriff's Posse staged a rodeo while at Camp Barkeley.

the new outfit. The Army selected 678 men to form the 12th Maintenance Battalion, which then became a part of the 12th Armored Division. The battalion was formed in July 1942 at Camp Perry, Ohio, where the men had their basic military training. The Harvester men then went to Camp Campbell, Kentucky, where they formed a portion of the original complement of the division when it was activated on September 15, 1942. Over time many of the original men were detached from the Harvester Battalion, later renamed the 134th Ordnance Maintenance Battalion, to form cadres for other units, and new replacements filled the void. Until the end of the war, however, the Harvester Battalion maintained its unit identity and played a key role in keeping the 12th Armored Division in fighting trim.[56]

In spite of their difficult training, the men of the 12th still found time for recreation and entertainment. Service clubs on the base provided weekly concerts, with entertainment ranging from exotic Spanish dancing to ballets and classical music productions featuring the works of Brahms, Mendelssohn, and Schubert. The latest movies from Hollywood also showed at base theaters, and the base service clubs often sponsored dances and bingo nights. Soldiers who complained of nothing to do simply chose not to find anything to do.[57]

During the first part of the year, a group of talented young Hellcats decided to write and produce a Broadway-style musical for the entertainment of the soldiers. The production, entitled "Hellcat Holiday," opened at Base Theater Number 1 on April 18, 1944, and played for several days at Camp Barkeley before going on the road to other Army bases in the area. The all-soldier cast of one hundred men was augmented by a number of local girls, either students at Hardin-Simmons College or wives of

Hellcats loading their vehicles on a train, preparing to move out.

soldiers. The fast-paced two-act play, featuring skits in addition to songs, was a big success in the Army camps, as well as for the civilian population of Abilene, when the play showed at the Abilene High School auditorium on May 2. All the music for the production was composed and arranged by GI musicians, and the 12th Armored Division orchestra backed up the singers.[58]

On Saturday and Sunday, June 3-4, 1944, the Hellcats of the 12th, along with the Taylor County Sheriff's Posse, staged a rodeo at the West Texas Fair Grounds Arena. Soldiers and civilian cowboys alike participated in the rodeo, which included such events as bareback bronc riding, soldier bull riding, and cowboy bull riding. Corporal Hubert Taylor, Jr. (Hillsboro, Ohio), a member of Company B, 119th Armored Engineer Battalion, placed first in three of the four events he entered, winning money in the soldier bareback bronc riding, soldier bull riding, and cowboy bull riding. Another soldier, Staff Sergeant John Davis (Vine Grove, Kentucky) of the 495th Armored Field Artillery, also placed in the money, taking third place in the soldier bull riding event. The rodeo was one of many events that epitomized the friendly relationship that existed between the people of Abilene and the soldiers of Camp Barkeley.[59]

In March 1944 the division received an infusion of new soldiers when the Army cancelled one of its many educational programs. The Army Specialized Training Program, or ASTP, was designed to provide the rapidly expanding Army with well-trained specialists in such areas as engineering, medicine, veterinary medicine, and foreign languages. Young men who scored highly on aptitude tests were assigned to a number of colleges and universities throughout the country where they embarked on a rigorous course of instruction designed to give the men a four-year college education in two years. In early 1944, however-er, the Army decided to cancel the program, and the young college students were assigned to divisions in combat or preparing for combat.

> We were loaded up in the back of a truck and driven maybe a mile or so to a row of tar-paper shacks built out of plywood. Good grief! They were pretty sorry-looking buildings. They said, 'This is your barracks.'
> Staff Sergeant F. George Hatt
> A Company, 17th Armored
> Infantry Battalion

During the last part of March 1944, approximately 1,300 ASTP men came to Camp Barkeley where they were integrated into the 12th Armored Division. After being classified as to their skills and aptitudes, the men were assigned to units within the division. Most of the men, who thought they were going to receive college degrees and officer's commissions, ended up as privates in the infantry or the tank battalions.[60]

During the week beginning Sunday, June 11, 1944, the entire 12th Armored Division went to the field for an extensive test conducted by officers of the Army Ground Forces. The purpose of the test was to determine if the division was ready for combat. In the midst of the combat preparation testing, for some inexplicable reason, the XXIII Corps Headquarters decided to hold a garrison inspection of the 12th Armored Division cantonment area. The inspectors were displeased with the appearance of the division's area and required the division to return to Camp Barkeley to clean up the area.

Incredible as it may seem, the soldiers were pulled out of a test that would determine their fitness to go into combat. The men went back to Camp Barkeley where they swept and mopped their living quarters until they were spotless, then they returned to the maneu-

Major General Carlos Brewer

The first and longest-serving commanding general of the 12th Armored Division was Major General Carlos Brewer. Born in Western Kentucky in 1890, Brewer attended public schools in Mayfield, Kentucky, and attended West Kentucky College before entering the United States Military Academy at West Point in 1909. Graduating in 1913, Second Lieutenant Brewer traveled to Fort Sam Houston at San Antonio, Texas, where he joined the 3rd Artillery Regiment.

After serving on the Texas border with Mexico for three years, he received orders to West Point where he served as a mathematics instructor for the next five years, missing any chance of a combat assignment during the First World War. Then Brewer went to Hawaii where he joined the 8th Artillery Regiment, spent two years in Denver before attending the Field Artillery School in 1926-27, and graduated first in his class from the Command and General Staff College at Fort Leavenworth, Kansas.

General Carlos Brewer, commanding officer of the 12th Armored Division from its activation in September 1942 until August 1944.

At Fort Sill, Oklahoma, he became director of the Gunnery Department of the Field Artillery School. While at Fort Sill, then-Major Brewer developed a radically new artillery fire direction technique that provided direction for an entire battalion. The battalion fire direction concept became widely used throughout the Army and proved to be instrumental in bringing effective artillery fire on the enemy during World War II.

Brewer was promoted to Major General in August 1942, a month before the activation of the division. After supervising the training of the division for two years, General Brewer was relieved as commanding officer on August 16, 1944, due to a War Department regulation that generals commanding divisions must be under fifty years of age. Denied the command of a division, General Brewer served as commander of the 46th Group Artillery, supporting the 7th Army in Europe.

After the war General Brewer became Professor of Military Science at Ohio State University, a position he held until his retirement from the Army in 1950.[62]

ver area for a continuation of the combat testing exercise. The men were extremely upset at what they perceived as petty and idiotic behavior on the part of corps personnel, and consequently the division did not acquit itself well in the all-important testing. The division failed its combat readiness test.[61]

General Brewer instituted an enthusiastic training program designed to correct the deficiencies discovered by the umpires, as the division awaited another chance to prove itself. On July 7 the entire division participated in a massive vehicle march to nearby Camp Bowie, near Brownwood, Texas, where a second inspection took place beginning on July 9. This time the Hellcats were up to the task. In a five-day exercise, continuing day and night, the armored men of the 12th performed well, earning high praise from Major General Louis A. Craig, commanding general of the XXIII Corps. General Craig commented favorably on the discipline and fine spirit exhibited during the test by the junior officers and enlisted men of the division. After passing the test with flying colors, the Hellcats returned to Camp Barkeley to await their travel orders.[63]

The combat readiness test behind them, the Hellcats began their preparation for overseas movement. Soldiers had wills drawn up, made sure their insurance was in order, and provided allotments for dependents left in the states. All the men of the division worked long hours packing away weapons and crating up all the division property. On July 20 the division received its readiness date, and on July 28 the division transferred all soldiers in the hospital to other units. On August 8 the long-awaited movement orders arrived, and on August 12 all leaves and furloughs were cancelled.

On August 15, 1944, the Hellcats held a division review to honor Major General Carlos Brewer, the man who commanded the division and directed its training since the division's activation. On the following day General Brewer was relieved of command, and Major General Douglas T. Greene assumed command of the division.

"As you reach the top of the gangplank and set foot upon the ship, you felt a very queer feeling coming over you. You didn't have time to say a prayer, but you did think of home and begin to realize more than ever what it had meant to you and gave a guess to the day you would be back again."

Corporal Vincent George Brackett, 714th Tank Battalion.

CHAPTER 4

Movement to France and the First Battle

At the end of August the long-awaited movement of the division began. An advanced detachment of troops under the command of newly-promoted Brigadier General Riley F. Ennis departed Camp Barkeley for Camp Shanks, New York. As the remainder of the Hellcats prepared to leave Texas, they removed the shoulder patches from their uniforms in an effort to conceal their identity from prying eyes along their journey. The Army, and the men of the 12th, took the secrecy of troop movements very seriously.

On September 5, 1944, the bulk of the division began boarding trains of the Atchison, Topeka, & Santa Fe Railway at the small community of View, Texas, four miles south of the main gate of Camp Barkeley. Some of the men went aboard crowded troop sleeper cars, while others enjoyed the relative luxury of Pullman sleepers, with larger and more comfortable beds. As the trains pulled out of the View station they began chugging their way east and then north. The train trip was long and hot, as there was no air conditioning on the

The Marine Raven was one of the ships that transported the Hellcats to England.

The Hellcats called their temporary camp near Tidworth, England "Windmill Hill."

cars, and anyone who has been there can tell you that Texas in September is hot. Unable to sleep in the heat, many of the Hellcats participated in non-stop crap and card games, with a great amount of money changing hands daily.

Arriving at Camp Shanks in New York some three days later, many of the Hellcats took advantage of eighteen-hour passes to explore the delights of New York City. After about a week in Camp Shanks, the division boarded ferries, which took the men across the Hudson River and on to the New York Port of Embarkation.[64]

During their short stay in England, many soldiers visited London and other cities.

The entire division of some eleven thousand men could not all be crammed into any one ship, so the Hellcats traveled to Europe on three separate troopships, with different battalions on each vessel. The men began boarding their transport ships tied up to the piers in New York Harbor on September 19, the same day Major General Roderick Allen assumed command of the division. Loaded down with backpacks, duffel bags, gas masks, musette bags, and miscellaneous extraneous gear virtually guaranteed to cause a hernia, the troops marched up gangplanks onto the decks of the ships that would take the division to its destination across the Atlantic.

The three ships assigned to the 12th Armored Division were the USS *General T. H. Bliss*, the SS *Empress of Australia*, and the USS *Marine Raven*. The *General T. H. Bliss*, built by the Kaiser Company in Richmond, California, was commissioned into the service of the Navy in February 1944 and could carry 3,522 embarked soldiers in addition to her crew. During the war she made numerous troop-carrying voyages to both the Pacific and European theaters. The *Empress of Australia* was laid down as a passenger liner in 1912 for the German transatlantic passenger trade but was ceded to Great Britain at the end of World War I. The Canadian Pacific line then bought the ship and renamed her the *Empress of Australia.* In 1939 she served as the Royal Yacht and carried King George VI and Queen

The M-7 self propelled 105-millimeter howitzer was the artillery piece of the division.

The division received new halftracks during their brief stop in England.

Elizabeth from England to Canada. After the outbreak of the war, she became a troopship, a function she filled for the duration of the war. The *Marine Raven*, built in 1944 in Chester, Pennsylvania, was a troop transport operated by the United States Maritime Commission and had a troop capacity of 2,439 men.

Once aboard his ship, each overburdened soldier laboriously wound his way down into the bowels of his ship, where he received his bunk and mess assignments. After the division was safely stowed aboard the ships that would take it to Europe, the convoy formed up and got underway. The holds of the ships were hot and stuffy, but the men were not allowed on the main deck until the ships had cleared New York Harbor. Once at sea, the men were permitted to leave their berthing areas, where bunks were stacked four and five high.[65]

The crossing was fairly uneventful, although there was the ever-present danger of attack by German U-boats. A number of the Hellcats volunteered to man some of the ship's guns and were able to spend a good bit of time above decks, in the fresh air. Other men spent their time down below, reading, sleeping, and shooting craps. With so many men on board each ship, up to five thousand on the

Empress of Australia, a great amount of time was spent standing in chow lines. For hours on end the soldiers stood in line, slowly moving forward, until they finally arrived at the serving line, received their metal trays of food, clammy with dampness and slopped with unappetizing navy beans or other such fare. After being served the soldiers sought an uncrowded bench upon which to sit and eat.

Most of the division's vehicles went from England to France on LSTs (Landing Ship, Tank).

Some men spent as much time as they could up on the main deck, to get away from the foul-smelling, claustrophobic conditions below. While out in the open the men could see the great number of other ships in the convoy, extending out as far as the eye could see in every direction. Every few minutes the entire convoy changed directions, as it zigzagged to avoid an ambush by German U-boats. The constant rocking and pitching of the ship made some of the Hellcats a little woozy, although the convoy did not encounter seas rough enough to incur serious seasickness.

At last the long voyage ended, and on Sunday the first of October, after eleven days at sea, the Hellcats sighted land, passing through the same Irish Sea in which the Lusitainia had been sunk thirty years earlier. As the ships of the convoy eventually found their berths in the harbor at Liverpool, the Hellcats once again loaded up all their gear, and the men in their seemingly endless lines wound their way up to the main deck, then down the gang plank to dry land once again.

Once ashore, the men of the division boarded English trains for various temporary staging areas—Hungerford, Chilbolton, and Southport. The Hellcats remained there for a few days before moving on to Camp R-4, at the town of Tidworth on the Salisbury Plain near Andover. While most of the division billeted in the former British

Many of the Hellcats went ashore in France from LCIs (Landing Craft, Infantry).

Army post called Tidworth Barracks, the three infantry battalions went to a tent camp nearby called Pennings Camp.

Here the American boys became acquainted with life in Merry Old England, as they learned to appreciate fish and chips and warm beer during trips to the nearby communities of Andover and Salisbury. Many a pint of ale or bitter went down the hatch during and between games of darts in England's legendary pubs. Many Hellcats also made their way to London to see the delights of that most famous of English cities.[66]

Tidworth was not the most comfortable or elegant place in England. It was strictly a temporary Army camp on a muddy plain, and the men soon referred to the place as "Windmill Hill" because of the high winds in the area. The camp consisted of row after row of eight-man pyramidal tents, with a few Quonset huts for battalion offices, mess facilities, and showers. Many other units had utilized the large camp before moving on to France during and after the D-Day landings of June 6, 1944, and with the heavy vehicle and foot traffic and frequent rains, the place was a sea of mud.

The first order of business for the soldiers was to construct wooden sidewalks so the men could navigate about the camp without being knee-deep in mud all the time. The next order of business was to find stoves to heat the cold, damp tents. Then there was a constant struggle to find enough fuel for the stoves, either wood or coal. The men were issued coal, but the ration was only one pound of coal per man per week. In some of the tents the freezing Hellcats burned up a month's supply of coal in a night. Then they had to resort to "midnight requisitioning," or theft, to ensure an adequate supply.[67]

Cutting down live trees was unlawful in England, although the men were permitted to chop up fallen trees. As a result, a few trees that seemed healthy suddenly fell over during the dark of the night. Some soldiers came up with the idea of burning the cardboard tubes that tank and artillery shells came in. The cardboard made a good

The Division was assigned to the Seventh Army, commanded by Lieutenant General Alexander Patch.

fire, but the tubes were coated with creosote as a water repellant, and the creosote made a smelly, smoky fire that sickened some of the soldiers.[68]

During their short stay at Tidworth, the Hellcats continued with a light training routine and suffered their first overseas casualty. Private First Class Robert I. Ervin of Company A, 17th Armored Infantry Battalion died on Sunday October 29, 1944, as a result of a training accident. A defective round from an 81-millimeter mortar struck him as his unit conducted maneuvers on the Salisbury Plain. He is buried at the U.S. National Cemetery at Cambridge, England, the first of many Hellcats to be laid beneath foreign soil.[69]

While in England the division received new vehicles—peeps (jeeps), trucks, weapons carriers, half-tracks, M-7 self-propelled artillery pieces, and tanks. The tank mechanics were delighted to see their new tanks had the big Ford V-8 engines, much stronger and more reliable than the radial engines of the tanks at Camp Barkeley. After the vehicles arrived, the training tempo increased, with frequent trips to the firing ranges. During this time the new commanding officer, Major General Roderick Allen, became acquainted with the officers and men of the division.[70]

General Roderick Random Allen

General Roderick Allen became the division commander shortly before the Hellcats sailed for Europe.

Roderick Allen, commander of the 12th Armored Division during its combat service, was a credit to his state, his country, and the Army. Born in Marshall, Texas, on January 29, 1894, he grew up in nearby Palestine. After completing high school, young Allen attended Texas A&M, graduating in 1915 with a Bachelor of Science in Agriculture. He was a member of the Corps of Cadets and was the senior cadet major during his senior year. As the honor graduate of his class, he received a direct commission into the U.S. Army Cavalry. In April 1917 he married Maydelle Campbell, daughter of a former governor of Texas.

Nicknamed "Red" because of his hair, Allen was a large man and a natural athlete. After attending the cavalry service school at Fort Leavenworth, Kansas, he was assigned to the 16th Cavalry Regiment and served on the Mexican Border during the spring and summer of 1917. In October of that year, he was promoted to captain and went to France with the 3rd Cavalry, where he commanded a troop and later a squadron. His duties included command of a remount station and a veterinary hospital.

Returning to the states after the end of World War I, Allen attended service schools and experienced the normal duties of an officer in the small peacetime Army. After serving in staff positions in Washington, D.C., he became operations and training officer in the newly-organized 1st Armored Division in July 1940. In September 1944 Major General Allen assumed command of the 12th Armored Division. While commanding the division during six months of combat, General Allen earned the Bronze Star, Silver Star, Legion of Merit and Distinguished Service Medal, as well as the French Legion of Honor and Croix de Guerre with palm.

After the war, General Allen served in the occupation Army in Germany and was a staff officer with the United Nations command during the Korean War. He received an honorary doctorate from Texas A&M in 1949 and retired in 1954 after thirty-seven years of faithful service to his country. He resided in Washington, D.C., until his death in 1970 and was laid to rest in Arlington National Cemetery.[71]

Finally it was time to pack up and head to France. On November 8, Hellcat drivers began moving some of the vehicles from Tidworth to the marshalling areas on the east coast of England. On November 9 General Allen and his advance party departed, and the remainder of the division followed over the next few days. Some of the men went in their tanks, half-tracks and M-7s, while others traveled by

On December 5, 1944, this gun fired the division's first shot in the war. Number 2 gun, Battery A, 493rd Armored Field Artillery Battalion.

train. At Dorchester, Weymouth, and Southampton the Hellcats once again boarded ships, this time for a much shorter voyage, just across the English Channel. Tanks and other vehicles went aboard LSTs (Landing Ship, Tank) which were large flat-bottomed craft with a clam-shell-like bow that opened to allow vehicles to drive on and off. Some of the men boarded the LSTs, while other Hellcats boarded troop transports such as the British *HMS Antenor*.[72]

Once aboard ship and underway, the drivers of some of the vehicles on the LSTs became friendly with the sailors on the ship, who informed the Hellcat drivers that there were large quantities of fruit cocktail in the ship's galley, or kitchen. Many of the drivers loaded up their half-tracks with one-gallon cans of fruit cocktail, while the sailors conveniently looked the other way.[73]

The trip across the choppy English Channel took only a few hours, but that was long enough for many of the men in the flat-bottomed LSTs to become sick. As the ships neared Le Havre, the destination of the division, the ships hove to and dropped anchor. An immense amount of shipping was waiting to unload, and the Hellcats had to wait their turn before coming into the port. Many of the dock facilities had also been destroyed, which further delayed the unloading process. While the flat-bottomed LSTs could ease up to the shore and disgorge their cargoes directly onto the beach, the deeper-drafted vessels, such as HMS *Antenor*, could not do the same. The men on the *Antenor* had to climb down the side of the ship on rope cargo nets and enter smaller Landing Craft, Infantry (LCI) which then relayed the men to the beach. That process was, of course, very laborious and time consuming. Some of the vessels had to wait three days before eventually unloading their cargoes of men, vehicles, and supplies.[74]

Once the men unloaded from their vessels, some marched a short distance and then climbed into waiting trucks, while other men drove their tanks, halftracks, and other vehicles away from the port area. The port and city of Le Havre had suffered utter devastation. Only silent, ghastly hulks of buildings remained, as mute testimony to the destructiveness of war. Sadly, much of the destruction was caused by American bombers and naval gunfire, in an effort to drive the German defenders from the strategic port and adjacent city. Some Frenchmen were very bitter toward the Americans for destroying their town while liberating it from German occupation.

> *I threw myself across a bed in my command post for a couple of hours of sleep. I was awakened suddenly at daylight by a noise and from being bounced in bed. An enemy 88mm shell had cut through the corner of the building and grazed the bed frame as it went underneath my bed. What an introduction to combat!*
> Captain Carl J. Helton
> Company A, 17th Armored
> Infantry Battalion

After passing quickly through the rubble-filled streets of Le Havre, the various units of the division began assembling a few miles inland in the vicinity of the town of Auffey. The division headquarters was set up in a large and imposing Norman chateau, known as the Chateau de Bosmelet. Many of the men stayed in the chateau, while other billeted in outlying buildings and in tents set up in the area.[75]

While awaiting orders at Auffey, the Hellcats made the best of their situation. Not knowing how long they would be there, some men scrounged lumber and built lean-tos or crude huts, while others found straw to use as bedding in order to get off of the damp and often muddy ground. Soldiers also went into the nearby town of Auffey, or visited neighboring farms, and exercised their high school French while trading with the local residents for fresh eggs and bread. While at Auffey the Hellcats also became acquainted with the

A series of forts such as this one comprised sections of the Maginot Line captured by the Hellcats.

apple cider that was a product of the local apple orchards, as well as French wine produced from the local vineyards.

After spending Thanksgiving at Auffey, the Hellcats finally received their marching orders. The division was assigned to the Seventh Army, commanded by Lieutenant General Alexander Patch, and on November 29 the Hellcats began advancing toward the front. Passing through the historic First World War battlefields of Soissons, Verdun, and Rheims, the division traveled east and a little south, and by December 1 the division headquarters had established a command post in the town of Luneville after a three-hundred mile road march. Luneville had been the scene of fierce fighting earlier in the war, and the Hellcats saw evidence of that fighting in the form of many burned out and destroyed German and American tanks, as well as the bodies of dead German soldiers. While at Luneville, the 572nd Anti-aircraft Artillery (Automatic Weapons) Battalion and the 827th Tank Destroyer Battalion joined the division.[76]

On December 5 the division was attached to XV Corps, and on that same day the Hellcats received orders to move out from

The 92nd Cavalry Reconnaissance Squadron prepares for an attack near the Maginot Line in December.

Luneville to Kirrberg. During this move, as would occur many times later on, the 92nd Cavalry Reconnaissance Squadron and the three armored field artillery battalions were temporarily removed so that they could support other units.

While the artillery was detached, it fired the first shots of the division in the war against Germany. At 4:38 p.m. on December 5, 1944, the number 2 gun section of Battery A, 493rd Armored Field Artillery Battalion fired the division's first shot—in support of the 44th Infantry Division near Weisslingen, France.[77]

On December 6 the division received orders to begin relieving the 4th Armored Division on the front lines in the vicinity of Domfessel. It was generally acknowledged that the 4th was the premier armored division in the European Theater, and the favorite division of General George Patton. Many of the Hellcats felt a sense of pride upon taking the place of such a respected division, while other Hellcats wondered what they were getting into, with such a green, untested division replacing the experienced tankers of the 4th.

The 12th completed the relief of the 4th Armored Division by the morning of December 8, and the division's next assignment was to support an attack by the 26th Infantry Division. The XV Corps, including the 26th and the 12th, was to breach the Maginot Line on the French frontier and continue attacking and advancing to the Siegfried Line across the border in Germany.[78]

The French built the Maginot line, named for War Minister Andre Maginot, during the 1930s in an effort to protect France from German invasion as had occurred in 1914. The Maginot Line was a series of fortresses, complete with underground showers, living and sleeping quarters, kitchens, and ammunition storage. The fortresses extended several stories under ground, and different forts were connected to each other by underground tunnels. These massive fortifications barely slowed the German assault of France in 1940, as the Germans simply went around the line by invading Belgium. The Germans then captured the Maginot Line from the rear.

The combat debut of the 12th Armored Division occurred in two separate phases, with a pause in between. The first fighting occurred during December 7-15, and the second phase took place during December 19-25. During the night of December 7, elements of the 17th Armored Infantry Battalion moved into the French town of Bining, relieving a battalion of the 26th Infantry Division. At that time the Americans controlled the southern half of Bining, while the Germans held the other half. The doughboys of the 17th made their approach to Bining on foot, at night, soaked to the skin after a driving rain, with mud up to their boot-tops. Carrying weapons, ammunition, bedrolls and musette bags, while slogging through the mud, the men quickly became fatigued. It was a feeling with which they would become very accustomed. After making their way quietly into the town, the Hellcats crowded into houses and barns to get out of the cold weather.[79]

In the evening of Friday, December 8, elements of Combat Command A launched a limited attack to seize the high ground overlooking the village of Singling. Before daylight the following morning the Hellcats resumed the attack and captured Singling and a portion of the surrounding countryside.

On that same morning of December 9, the 17th Armored Infantry Battalion occupied all of the town of Bining, meeting no opposition. The infantrymen then advanced toward the nearby military installation known as Bining Barracks. Meeting determined German resistance, the 17th Armored Infantry and the 43rd Tank Battalion con-

Lt. Col. Montgomery Meigs, commanding the 23rd Tank Battalion, was among the first of the Hellcats to be killed in action. He received a posthumous Silver Star.

ducted a full-scale assault of the barracks, killing or driving away the German defenders. By that night, all of Bining Barracks was in American hands, and many of the green troops of the division had received their baptism into battle.[80]

On the morning of Sunday, December 10, Combat Command A attacked the town of Rohrbach, located only one kilometer north of Bining Barracks. Meeting no resistance in the town, the soldiers continued their push north toward the Maginot Line. After capturing higher ground north of Rohrbach, the doughboys of the 17th Armored Infantry received a German artillery barrage and had to pull back a little and dig in.[81]

On December 10 the fighting Hellcats captured several pillboxes and other buildings comprising a portion of the Maginot Line defenses. The objective of the division was the town of Bettwiller, a small town on the German side of the border. On the morning of the 11th as the 23rd Tank Battalion moved into position to provide support for the assaulting infantry, the American tanks came under heavy fire. Lieutenant Colonel Montgomery C. Meigs, the battalion commander, was leading from the front and had just located the enemy guns that had stopped the American advance when he was struck and killed by an enemy shell.[82]

Elements of the division made three separate attacks on December 12, which resulted in the capture of Bettwiller, the division objective, as well as the adjacent towns of Guising and Hoelling. After consolidating the division's positions, the Hellcats held in place for a few days before being relieved by other American units. The combat veterans of the 12th Armored Division moved to the rear for a few days to rest, rehabilitate, replace their losses, and absorb the lessons they had learned in combat.

This first combat action, a series of skirmishes, cost the division the lives of six officers and thirty-seven enlisted men. An additional sixteen officers and 141 enlisted men suffered wounds. During a brief period of rest away from the front lines, the wounded received Purple Heart medals, and the first Silver Star medals were awarded posthumously to Lieutenant Colonel Montgomery Meigs and Captain Carl Adams, both of the 23rd Tank Battalion.[83]

*"I was still very concerned about surrendering.
I hoped I'd saved a life, but then how many
had I endangered? This bothered me then and it
still does today. The Germans gave us some
black bread for lunch. That stuff tasted like dried,
burned shingle. Most of us threw it away,
thinking we would be receiving food later on.
We soon found out that was no snack, it was
breakfast, dinner and supper. That black bread
soon began to taste like chocolate cake."*

1st Lieutenant Marvin Drum, Company A, 17th Armored Infantry Battalion.

CHAPTER 5

The Nightmare of Herrlisheim

On December 16, 1944, the German Army launched its largest offensive since the Allied invasion of France at Normandy. In a campaign that became known as the Battle of the Bulge, Hitler ordered his western army to attack through the Ardennes Forest and fall on the previously quiet section of the American line in Luxembourg and Belgium. The massive German attack caught the Americans by surprise, and initially the enemy forces made great gains against the U.S. troops.

As the American Army forces scrambled to contain the German offensive, General George Patton's Third Army, which had been south of the area of attack, had to pull out of its lines and march northward to confront the Germans. Patton's movement northward

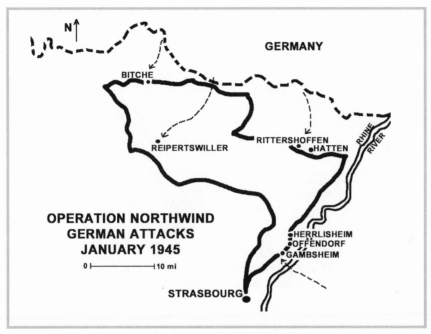

GERMANY

BITCHE

REIPERTSWILLER

RITTERSHOFFEN
HATTEN

RHINE RIVER

OPERATION NORTHWIND
GERMAN ATTACKS
JANUARY 1945
0 |————————| 10 mi

HERRLISHEIM
OFFENDORF
GAMBSHEIM

STRASBOURG

Operation Northwind consisted of four distinct attacks along the Seventh Army front.

meant that the Seventh Army, the parent organization of the 12th Armored Division, had to then shift northward as well and cover the area vacated by the Third Army. As a result, the Seventh Army ended up covering twice as much territory as it could reasonably be expected to do. The front lines in the Seventh Army area were stretched dangerously thin, held primarily by inexperienced units.

While initially taking the American forces by surprise, the Battle of the Bulge eventually became a great Allied victory, as the United States Army regrouped and counterattacked, and eventually destroyed or captured a major portion of the German Army involved in the campaign. Even before the conclusion of the ill-fated Battle of the Bulge — ill-fated from the German perspective, that is — Hitler and his military planners came up with an operation as a counter to the American victory. The massive amount of press coverage given the Battle of the Bulge during the war, and the great number of histories written about it after the war, completely overshadow the very significant subsequent battles of Operation Nordwind, the last great German offensive on the Western Front.

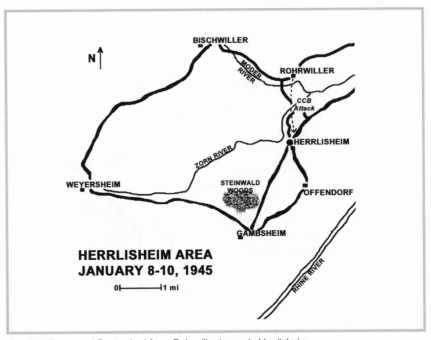

Combat Command B attacked from Rohrwiller towards Herrlisheim.

Operation Nordwind, or Northwind, grew out of the German knowledge that the Allied lines south of the Battle of the Bulge area had been stretched thin to allow Patton's Third Army to move north. The Germans planned to attack in the French region of Alsace, a level plain lying between the Vosges Mountains and the German border at the Rhine River. An attack in this area, where the American lines were weakest, would accomplish three objectives. First, by attacking in a new area, the Germans would relieve the pressure on other German units involved in the Battle of the Bulge. Secondly, the Germans hoped to annihilate the dangerously extended U.S. Seventh Army, inflicting severe casualties on the American soldiers. Finally, a German penetration in Alsace would join up with the German Nineteenth Army that had a lodgment in France in the vicinity of Colmar, south of Strasbourg.[84] The German High Command believed a successful campaign in Western France would breathe new life into the war on the Western Front.

The German offensive of Operation Nordwind consisted of four distinct attacks along the Seventh Army front in the Alsace region

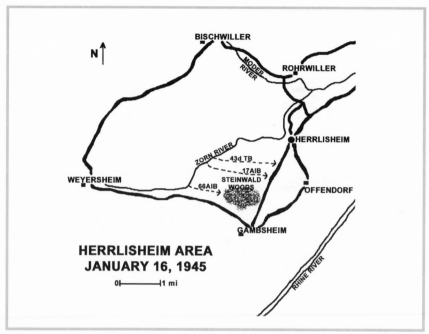

66th AIB attacked Steinwald, while 43rd Tank Bn and 17th AIB attacked toward Offendorf.

of France. The first attack occurred in the area of the fortress of
Bitche, beginning on the night of December 31, 1944. The
Germans launched their second attack in the vicinity of
Reipertsweiller in the Hardt Mountains. The third attack struck the
Hatten and Rittershoffen area on the Alsatian Plain, while the final
attack crossed the Rhine River in the Herrlisheim-Gambsheim
area. It was this final attack that concerned the 12th Armored
Division.

German Army forces crossed the Rhine River on the morning of
Saturday, January 5, 1945, at the small French village of Gambsheim,
about ten miles north of Strasbourg. The German 553rd
Volksgrenadier Division, reinforced with armored and commando
units, then attacked the weak American positions on the west, or
French, side of the Rhine. The German attack struck scattered and
disorganized elements of the American 42nd Infantry Division, which
had no organic armor, artillery, signal, or transportation units. The
unsupported U.S. rifle battalions made local counterattacks against
the German intrusion, but their valiant attempts to drive the

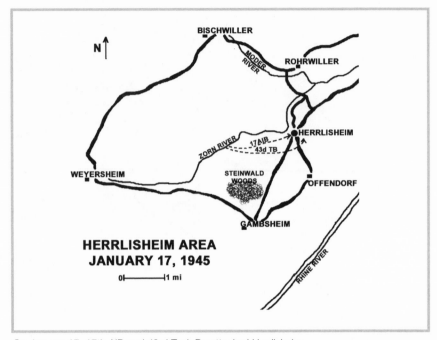

On January 17, 17th AIB and 43rd Tank Bn attacked Herrlisheim.

Germans back across the river failed. By nightfall on January 5 the Germans had established a firm bridgehead at least five miles long and two miles deep on the west side of the Rhine River.[85]

As the German intrusion gushed northward from Gambsheim to Offendorf and Herrlisheim, the American VI Corps commander, Major General Edward H. Brooks, scrambled to contain the spreading menace. On January 6 General Brooks moved a few infantry battalions of the 79th Infantry Division to the Gambsheim area, but they could not halt the German advance. Lieutenant General Jacob L. Devers, commander of the Sixth Army Group, decided to send in his last reserve unit, the 12th Armored Division.

General Brooks ordered General Allen to send one combat command to assist in halting the German advance. Combat Command B of the 12th, under the command of Colonel Charles V. Bromley, moved to the town of Hochfelden , arriving there on the morning of January 7, at which time it was attached to the 79th Infantry Division, VI Corps. Combat Command B at that time consisted of the 56th Armored Infantry Battalion, the 714th Tank Battalion, the 494th

714th Tank Battalion near Bischwiller approaching Herrlisheim.

Armored Field Artillery Battalion, and Company B of the 119th Armored Engineer Battalion.

On the morning of January 8, VI Corps headquarters ordered Combat Command B to attack the town of Herrlisheim from the north, giving the Hellcats only a few hours to prepare for the mission. The area of operations was a flat plain, bordered on the east by the Rhine River, crisscrossed by small rivers and canals, making it very difficult for tanks to operate. Roads in the area were built up higher than the surrounding countryside, giving excellent protection to the German defensive anti-tank guns, artillery and mortars, which could hide behind the elevated roads. This was also the coldest winter in many years, and the ground was frozen solid to a depth of a foot or more, making the rapid digging of foxholes exhausting if not impossible for the infantry. Conversely, tanks could and did go through the foot of frozen earth, and then became stuck in the underlying mud. In short, the terrain was unsuitable for the use of armor, and ideal for defense.[86]

As the Hellcats attacked Herrlisheim from the North, the French 2nd Armored Division was to make a simultaneous attack on the town of Gambsheim, about three miles to the south. VI Corps intel-

Aerial view of Herrlisheim.

ligence officers did not know the size of the enemy units on the west side of the Rhine but thought they were only a few hundred second-rate troops. Corps also had only a vague idea of the locations of the enemy units. Without having time to make an adequate reconnaissance or a detailed plan, Combat Command B moved in to attack.

> Suddenly, the basement door was blown open and a grenade thrown inside wounding a number of personnel. At that point, Major Logan decided to surrender the CP since the obvious alternative was death for all personnel present. As we came out of the CP under the flashlights and guns of enemy soldiers, I fully expected to be shot.
>
> Captain Carl J. Helton
> Company A, 17th Armored

Jumping off from the town of Rohrwiller, as the doughboys of the 56th Armored Infantry approached the town of Herrlisheim, they found that the bridges over the Zorn River were destroyed, so the tankers of the 714th Tank Battalion could not accompany the infantry. The riflemen slugged their way toward the town unsupported, while the tanks had to remain on the far side of the river. There was no provision for radio communications between the tankers and the infantry, a shortcoming that would have disastrous results.

Running into heavy German resistance, the 56th fought for hours in a waterworks plant just outside of Herrlisheim and remained in

66th AIB soldiers digging in near Herrlisheim with a knocked-out German tank in background.

the waterworks overnight. Resuming the offensive the next morning, the infantrymen of the 56th ran into stiff machinegun and mortar fire, which slowed their advance and inflicted heavy casualties. Finally advancing into the town late in the evening, the three rifle companies of the battalion became separated from each other and lost communications with battalion headquarters.

During the night of January 9, Battalion Headquarters of the 56th Armored Infantry Battalion sent a reconnaissance platoon with a radio to contact the infantry companies in Herrlisheim and to establish radio communications between the rifle companies and Battalion Headquarters. The patrol discovered several soldiers who had fled from the town, and the soldiers said all the Americans in the town had been cut off and surrounded. The reconnaissance patrol returned to its own lines without accomplishing its mission.

During the long night of January 9-10, German tanks roamed the streets of Herrlisheim, shooting into buildings at random. The iso-

Bodies of 66th AIB soldiers being recovered after American forces finally occupied the Herrlisheim area in February 1945.

lated infantry companies of the 56th Battalion spent a lonely, anxious night. Not knowing the fate of the Americans in Herrlisheim, the next morning the headquarters of Combat Command B ordered Company B, 714th Tank Battalion, to go to the town, locate whatever friendly units were still there, and withdraw from the town. Company B could muster only six tanks, four having been destroyed the previous day. Crossing a newly-constructed temporary bridge, the tanks entered the town just at daylight on the morning of the 10th.

Once the tanks had made their way into the town and contacted the infantry, the commander of Combat Command B changed his mind and ordered all units to stay in the town. During the morning a company of engineers, acting as infantry, entered the town to reinforce the depleted rifle companies. Later in the day additional American tanks entered the town, but the Germans subjected the town and its approaches to heavy shelling from artillery and anti-tank guns. The German fire destroyed several American tanks and killed and wounded many of the infantry. Combat Command B attempted to air-drop medical supplies to the men in the town, but the mission was unsuccessful due to poor visibility.

German artillery and mortar fire continued to take a toll on the Hellcats during the day, and late in the evening the combat commander changed his mind once again and ordered an immediate evacuation of the town. The soldiers in the town placed the wounded on the tanks, which then withdrew, with the remaining infantry covering the retreat. After pulling out of Herrlisheim, the tanks and infantry established a defensive position on the edge of the village of Rohrwiller, some two miles away.

Lt. Gen. Jacob Devers, commander of Sixth Army Group, confers with Lt. Gen. Alexander Patch, commander of the Seventh Army, during Operation Northwind.

The initial assault on Herrlisheim—an effort by VI Corps to reduce the German bridgehead on the French side of the Rhine — failed miserably. Many factors contributed to this failure. Combat Command B launched hurried, piecemeal attacks against an unknown enemy without having time to conduct proper reconnaissance or make adequate plans. There was a lack of coordination between VI Corps and the 79th Infantry Division, to whom Combat Command B was attached, and between the division and the combat command. Communications were inadequate at all levels, and the terrain worked against the Americans. Tanks can not go across rivers without bridges, and tanks are extremely vulnerable in towns, where enemy bazooka teams can sneak up and destroy them. The combination of all of these factors resulted in prohibitive losses in men and material of the 56th Armored Infantry Battalion and the 714th Tank Battalion.[87]

General Alexander Patch, commanding the U.S. Seventh Army, belatedly authorized the use of the remainder of the 12th Armored Division, along with the 36th Infantry Division, to contain and

Hellcats investigating a knocked-out German tank.

reduce the German positions on the west side of the Rhine, known by the Americans as the Gambsheim Bridgehead. On January 16 the Hellcats began their second major attack on the Herrlisheim area. The plan was for Combat Command B (56th Armored Infantry Battalion and 714th Tank Battalion) to again attack Herrlisheim from the north, while Combat Command A (17th and 66th Armored Infantry Battalions, the 43rd and 23rd Tank Battalions, and elements of the 119th Engineer Battalion) attacked from the south. The 66th Armored Infantry received orders to clear the area south of Herrlisheim, including a wooded area, while the 17th Armored Infantry was to liberate the town of Offendorf, about a mile and a half southeast of Herrlisheim. At the same time, a French division was again scheduled to attack Gambsheim from the south.[88]

Combat Command B was once more unable to get across the rivers and canals north of Herrlisheim, as German artillery commanded the approaches to the rivers and interfered with the efforts of the engineers to emplace temporary bridges. In the south, the 66th Armored Infantry Battalion attempted to clear a small forest called the Steinwald, or "Stone Forest," and ran into a meat-grinder.[89]

General Jacob Devers while commander of the Armored Force at Fort Knox in 1942.

The heavily wooded area of the Steinwald was about one thousand yards long and some two hundred yards wide. The mission of the 66th doughboys was to clear the woods of enemy troops, reported to be a couple of hundred Volksstrum, or second-rate, homeguard troops. The information on the enemy was wrong.

On the morning of January 16 the men of the 66th moved out to the attack at about 6 a.m. There was a deep snow, and many of the men wore white sheets or cheesecloth as camouflage. In the dark, foggy, pre-dawn, the lead soldiers of C Company, 66th Armored Infantry Battalion came upon a German outpost of three men, and one of the Germans got away and alerted his companions in the woods.

> *January 16, 1945 was a very bad day for us in C-66.*
> PFC Stephen J. Czecha
> Company C, 66th Armored
> Infantry Battalion

Company C approached the Steinwald across a plain as flat as a pool table. As the men neared the woods, German machineguns opened up, killing and wounding many soldiers, including the officers and squad leaders, in the first moments of the one-sided battle. The remaining men fell to the ground, into the snow, and fired back at the muzzle flashes as best they could. A scant seventy yards separated the prone GIs from the German machineguns just inside the tree line, and any movement from the Americans brought an immediate burst of German automatic fire. Anyone trying to rise immediately fell back down riddled with bullets.

During the course of the day, several American tanks came forward and tried to interpose themselves between Company C and the woods to rescue the pinned-down Hellcats, but German tanks and anti-tanks guns blasted the American tanks like ducks in a shooting gallery. The agony lasted for hours, from 6 a.m. until 3 p.m., at which time German soldiers came forward to strip the American dead, not realizing any were still alive. The doughboys who survived, wounded or whole, had lain in the snow, completely immobile, for hours. Many suffered frostbite, and none could walk unaided. Company C, 66th Armored Infantry Battalion was wiped out. Forty-eight men were killed, twenty more wounded, and fifty-two captured, many of whom suffered wounds.[90]

> The emotions felt, during those early morning hours before daybreak and leading into early afternoon, that very cold and snowy fateful day - 16 January 1945 - will long be remembered. The sight of the dead and dying comrades will be engraved in my mind for eternity.
>
> Paul W. Rice, Jr.
> Company C, 66th Armored

While the 66th endured its agony, the 17th Armored Infantry Battalion and the 43rd Tank Battalion moved out on their mission to capture Offendorf. In the confusion of the attack, enhanced by a heavy fog which severely limited visibility, the men of the Offendorf task force believed that friendly troops had successfully occupied the Steinwald. As the 17th and 43rd passed north of the woods, heading toward Offendorf, machinegun, mortar, and artillery fire slammed into the right flank of the American infantry and armored units. German 88-millimeter cannons, in the forest and dug in along the raised Gambsheim-to-Herrlisheim road, turned on the American tanks, making mincemeat of the Shermans. Tank after tank exploded as the accompanying infantry scrambled to dig holes for protection in the frozen earth. Within minutes twelve American tanks had

One of the 23rd Tank Battalion tanks destroyed during the Herrlisheim battle.

become blazing hulks, and the remainder withdrew from the battle-field. Later in the evening the infantry also pulled back.[91]

On the following morning Combat Command A changed its objective to the town of Herrlisheim, and the troops moved out well before daylight on Wednesday, January 17. As the infantry approached the southern outskirts of the town, more than two hundred German soldiers, in trenches just outside the village, surrendered to the Americans. The 17th quickly overran the initial German defenses and pushed their way into the town, encountering increasing resistance and counterattacks on their right flank, or from the east. The American advance ground to a halt less than halfway through the town.

The 43rd Tank Battalion, advancing separately from the infantry, entered the east edge of Herrlisheim, where the tankers quickly received heavy fire from German tanks and anti-tank guns. In very heavy and confused fighting during the day, the infantrymen took up defensive positions in the town, while the 43rd tank battalion, separated from the infantry, seemingly disappeared. Radio contact was lost, and for hours none of the tanks could be located.

It turned out that Combat Command A of the 12th Armored Division had run into not only the 553rd Volksgrenadier Division, but also a headlong attack of the German 10th SS Panzer Division, a well-equipped and very experienced Nazi unit. As the 43rd tanks made their way into town, they were overwhelmed by German tanks, anti-tank guns, and soldiers carrying panzerfaust anti-tank weapons. Concealed German anti-tank guns destroyed those tanks that attempted to move out onto the open plains east of Herrlisheim. During the terrible fighting of January 17, the German forces destroyed or captured twenty-nine American tanks, plus the twelve tanks destroyed on the previous day. The 43rd Tank Battalion lost every tank in its task force, as well as the battalion commander, Lieutenant Colonel Nicholas Novosel.[92]

As the 43rd Tank Battalion was being obliterated, the 17th Armored Infantry Battalion was having its own problems. After fighting their way into Herrlisheim, the Hellcats found themselves completely encircled by German infantry supported by Panther tanks of the 10th SS Panzer Division. The rifle companies of the 17th beat back numerous attacks, and requested reinforcements, which division headquarters did not send. During the night of Wednesday, January 17, more German troops and tanks entered Herrlisheim, and one by one they cut off and captured the American infantry platoons and companies. At about 4:00 a.m. on Thursday, January 18, with German tanks firing directly into his command post, Major James Logan, commander of the infantry battalion, surrendered his force. Not only the battalion commander, but also all the battalion headquarters personnel and the commanders of companies A and B, marched into captivity. Only a few small groups of 17th Infantry Battalion soldiers fought their way out of Herrlisheim and made their way back to the west to the U.S.-held village of Weyersheim.[93]

The tattered remnants of Combat Command A closed on Weyershiem and prepared to defend the town against the inevitable German attack. When the attack came during the afternoon of Friday, January 19, well-aimed artillery fire halted and turned back the German tanks and infantry.

During the night of January 19 and the early morning hours of January 20, the 36th Infantry Division, known as the "Texas Division" because it had been the Texas National Guard unit, moved into the positions held by the Hellcats. Elements of the 12th were temporarily attached to the 36th Division as the combined American force prepared defensive positions in the vicinity of Weyersheim. The Hellcats and Texans repelled several German attacks, inflicting heavy casualties on the enemy, sweet revenge for the battered Hellcats. On January 21 the 12th Armored Division departed Weyersheim and moved back away from the front lines for rehabilitation.

After the nightmare of the battle at Herrlisheim, the 12th Armored Division counted its losses (some 1,700 men killed, captured, or wounded), received and began training new replacements, and tried to learn from the experience. The battle in the Gambsheim Bridgehead was the bloodiest fighting the division endured during the course of the war and was a costly initiation into the brotherhood of combat veterans. Two battalions—the 43rd Tank Battalion and the 17th Armored Infantry Battalion—had been annihilated, with the loss of both battalion commanders as well as most of the men. The Hellcats emerged from the experience a humbled, much wiser, less innocent division, and vastly more experienced as a result of the hard lessons of January.[94]

*"The 92nd Reconnaissance Squadron
was out ahead of the task forces and we moved
as fast as possible, passing through one
wrecked town after another. Long lines of prisoners
were streaming to the rear as we caught the
enemy completely unprepared for this thrust
from the northwest. We passed long miles
of wrecked enemy convoys, artillery pieces, supply
wagons, and vehicles. All had been destroyed
by bombing and our fast-moving spearhead.
Dead horses and burning villages were everywhere."*

Tech Sergeant Carl Lyons, Company A, 17th Armored Infantry Battalion

CHAPTER 6

Colmar and the Race to the Rhine

The 12th Armored Division emerged from the battle at Herrlisheim much wiser and with a much greater appreciation for planning, reconnaissance, and communication. As the division absorbed the badly-needed new replacement troops, it moved off the line and into VI Corps reserve. There the men rested after their ordeal, repaired equipment, replenished their exhausted ammunition stocks, and trained the new recruits. On January 22, Seventh Army headquarters advised General Allen that control of the division had been temporarily transferred to the II French Corps of the First French Army. The Hellcats were to assist the French in clearing the Colmar Pocket.[95]

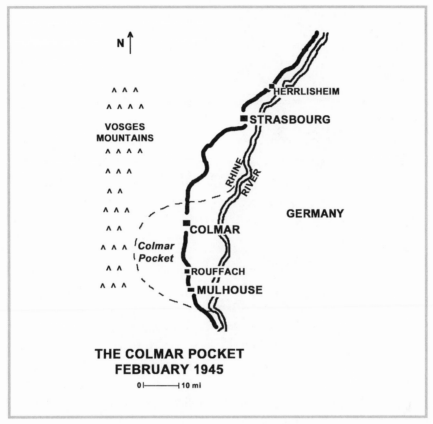

The Colmar Pocket was the last German-held territory in France.

The Colmar Pocket was a German-held 850-square-mile bulge or salient on the French side of the Rhine River south of Strasbourg. It was the last significant German stronghold in France. The major French city within the salient was Colmar, hence the name "Colmar Pocket." In January 1945 Lieutenant General Jacob Devers, commander of the 6th Army Group, ordered General de Lattre de Tassigney, commander of the First French Army, to eliminate the Colmar Pocket once and for all.

The reduction of the Colmar Pocket began on January 20 with a push from the south by the French I Corps. Kicking off their attack in a blinding snowstorm, the French made slow but steady progress, as the Germans fell back while launching their usual local counterat-

During the push to clear the Colmar Pocket, the Hellcats were assigned to the French First Army, commanded by General Jean-Marie de Lattre de Tassigny.

tacks. In the north the French II Corps attack began on January 22, achieving greater success.[96]

By February 2 the U.S. 28th Infantry Division and the French 5th Armored Division had completely cleared the northern outskirts of Colmar of all German presence, and were mopping up the last holdouts in the center and southern portions of the city. On the following day the 12th Armored Division, again under control of the U.S. XXI Corps, began moving their armored columns south, and passed through Colmar on February 4. Although they had done no fighting in the city, the French citizens greeted the Hellcats as liberators. Numerous young women, oblivious to the presence of dead Germans on the streets, brought bottles and pitchers of wine to the delighted American soldiers.

The Hellcats had little time to enjoy the festivities in town, as they pressed on through the crowded streets and immediately launched an attack on German positions to the south. In spite of heavy German artillery fire, two task forces of the division reached the Colmar Woods south of the city, where the entire division formed for an attack, working in conjunction with the U.S. 28th Infantry Division.

Working side-by-side with the soldiers from the "Bloody Bucket" division, the Hellcats raced to the south, bypassing strong points and exploiting enemy weak spots. The artillery battalions engaged targets on the Rhine River to the east as well as targets in the Vosges Mountains to the west, keeping the Germans guessing as to where

The Hellcats enter Colmar, February 4, 1945.

the shells would land next. Southwest of Colmar the division liberated another town called Herrlisheim, but without the bloody fighting of the first Herrlisheim. As the Hellcats moved swiftly forward against crumbling German resistance, dead horses in the roads often temporarily impeded their progress. These horses, used by the Germans to move their artillery pieces, were victims of Hellcat artillery fire.

As soon as the Hellcats secured one village, they moved on to the next. Task forces from the 12th met up with elements of the French I Corps in Rouffach during the early morning hours of February 5, and the two units completed clearing the town on the 6th, capturing a great number of German soldiers. Gueberschwihr and Pfaffenheim quickly fell to the irresistible 12th Armored Division, after which the Hellcats were told to move west and block the passages leading from the Vosges Mountains. The clearing of the Colmar Pocket was complete.[97]

The removal of the last remnants of the German Army from the sacred soil of France was an occasion of great celebration to the citizens of Colmar and the surrounding areas. The liberated French cel-

One of the numerous victory parades celebrating the liberation of Colmar.

ebrated with a victory parade in Colmar on February 8, and the 66th Armored Infantry Battalion represented the 12th Armored Division in the parade. The celebration on February 8 was only the first of many victory parades for the liberated inhabitants of Colmar and the surrounding region of Alsace. For their part in freeing Colmar, the soldiers of the 12th Armored Division were authorized to wear the Colmar Coat of Arms. The French also presented General Allen with the Legion of Honor and the Croix de Guerre with Palm. Additionally, the French awarded the Criox de Guerre to a dozen other officers and enlisted men of the division. Major General Milburn, commander of the XXI Corps, visited the division headquarters on February 9 and personally awarded General Allen the Bronze Star for his part in the campaign.[98]

The successful drive to eliminate the Colmar Pocket marked a period of transition for the 12th Armored Division. The division entered the conflict still a new, very inexperienced unit, badly shaken by the bloody initiation at Herrlisheim. During the drive from Colmar to Rouffach the division became a veteran outfit, perfecting the use of the highly mobile tank-infantry task forces, perhaps learn-

The 66th AIB represented the 12th Armored Division in this Colmar victory parade.

ing from the veteran 3rd and 28th Infantry Divisions alongside which the 12th Armored Division fought. As the Hellcats approached a town, some tanks would sweep around the town, blocking the roads on the far side, to prevent the arrival of reinforcements and to prevent the escape of the defenders. Then the infantry would clear the outskirts of the town, while the tanks and tank destroyers provided close support. If the infantry ran into machinegun nests or heavily fortified positions, the tanks would come forward and blast the opposition to bits.

The tank and armored infantry task forces honed their skills of planning quickly, moving rapidly, and communicating effectively. While moving forward, the artillery and tanks would fire on likely ambush or anti-tank gun locations, without waiting for the enemy to fire first. The task forces, smaller than combat commands, learned to pass through each other, quickly and efficiently, leapfrogging from one town to another. This valuable combat experience in mobile warfare prepared the Hellcats for the final battles that lay ahead.[99]

Following the Colmar victory celebration, the Hellcats received orders to move to the Saint Avold area, in Lorraine, about seventy miles to the north and west. There the Hellcats had the mission of

12th Armored tanks clearing the road south of Colmar.

maintaining a screen along the south side of the Maginot Line fortifications along the German border. Most of the division's artillery
units were attached to other divisions for the next few weeks.

During the last half of February the division was in XXI Corps
reserve and prepared to move out at short notice to repel any enemy
attacks, but it was not called on to perform that function. Instead,
the Hellcats rested, maintained their weapons and equipment,
rebuilt their depleted stocks of ammunition and supplies, and
received replacement troops to fill their losses. Squads, platoons,
and companies participated in tactical training and gained confi-
dence and proficiency by firing their weapons on improvised firing
ranges. The division received new vehicles to replace all those lost in
combat, and four M4A3-E8 tanks, the newest version with the high-
velocity 76-millimeter gun.

714th Tank Battalion attacking south of Colmar.

The Hellcats were billeted in the former French Army camp of Zimming Barracks and surrounding areas in the vicinity of Saint Avold. There the doughboys could take showers, watch movies, and have hot meals in a GI chow hall. While one combat command was on a three-hour alert status, soldiers in the other two combat commands could obtain passes to rest centers in Strasbourg, Paris, Nancy, Lyon, and the Riviera. Some lucky soldiers even received seven-day passes to London. The Hellcats thoroughly enjoyed their long-overdue but very welcome period of rest and relaxation.[100]

During the first part of March the Hellcat Division was generally held in XXI Corps reserve in the vicinity of Saint Avold, France, while the 92nd Cavalry Reconnaissance Squadron maintained a counter-reconnaissance screen along the Saar River and south of the Maginot Line. When no major breakthrough requiring the services of the Hellcats occurred, the division was given the job of supporting local

Hellcats moving through the streets of Herrlisheim near Colmar—the second Herrlisheim.

infantry attacks in the area of the Siegfried Line. These small probes into the enemy defenses by the 70th Infantry Division, supported by Combat Command A of the 12th, forced the Germans to withdraw from the village of Forbach. Combat Command A moved forward and occupied the town on March 5.[101]

A significant change to the division occurred on March 10, when twelve platoons of black infantry soldiers joined the Hellcats. The division formed the new soldiers into three rifle companies and attached the companies to the existing armored infantry battalions. The new companies were officially known as Seventh Army Provisional Rifle Companies 1, 2, and 3, but were informally referred to as Company D of each of the three infantry battalions. Although the black soldiers had scant infantry training when compared to their white counterparts, the black infantry made a generally good impression.

Sergeant Edward A. Carter, a black soldier from Los Angeles, California, in Company D, 56th Armored Infantry Battalion, was riding on a tank near Speyer, Germany, on March 23, 1945, when the tank column ran into heavy bazooka and small-arms fire. Sergeant Carter jumped off the tank on which he was riding and led three other men across an open field toward the source of the enemy fusillade. When his three companions were shot down by German fire, Carter continued alone until he was wounded five times and forced to seek cover. A German patrol then came out to his position, and Carter killed six of the enemy soldiers and captured the remaining two. Using his prisoners for a shield, Sergeant Carter returned to friendly lines where intelligence officers obtained valuable informa-

A Seventh Army light tank unit clearing the Colmar Pocket.

tion on enemy dispositions from the prisoners.

After the battle Captain Russell Blair, Sergeant Carter's white commanding officer, submitted paperwork nominating Carter for the Medal of Honor. The War Department downgraded the award to the Distinguished Service Cross, the Army's second highest award for valor. Many years later an Army review board determined that Carter's actions were worthy of the higher medal. Although Sergeant Carter died in 1963, Carter's family eventually received his Medal of Honor at a White House ceremony in 1997.[102]

During a time of strict racial segregation in the American armed forces, the 12th Armored Division had more black combat soldiers than any other unit in the Army. Although the black soldiers served in combat for only two months, they displayed a willingness to serve and to share all the hardships and dangers of their white comrades. Their courage and devotion to duty, and their general acceptance by white

Sergeant Edward A. Carter, Company D, 56th
AIB, received the Medal of Honor for his actions
near Speyer, Germany on March 23, 1945.

soldiers and officers, eased the way for full racial integration in the Army and the other services a few years later.

During a time of a relative lull in early March 1945, rumors began to circulate that the Hellcats would join the Third Army, commanded by flamboyant General George S. Patton. These rumors proved to be true when early in the morning of March 17 (St. Patrick's Day) the division received its marching orders. Patton had requested the Hellcats to spearhead his drive across Germany in an effort to secure bridges across the Rhine River. On March 17 the division was detached from the Seventh Army and assigned to the XX Corps of the Third Army, and moved out from Saint Avold to the vicinity of Sierck-les-Baines, some thirty-five miles to the northwest. From there the Hellcats crossed into Luxembourg, then entered Germany at Trier.

The German Army had a highly effective intelligence service, and it had a very good idea about which divisions belonged to which corps and armies. When the 12th Armored Division was taken from the Seventh Army and assigned to the Third Army, that necessarily made the Seventh Army weaker. In order to hide from the Germans where the weakness lay, the Hellcats had to remove their shoulder patches and paint over all the markings on their vehicles, so spies could not discern the identity of the unit. For that reason the 12th Armored Division became known as the "Mystery Division."[103]

After reaching its jump-off point, the 12th Armored Division became the armored spearhead of one wing of Patton's Third Army. General Patton ordered General Allen to advance as rapidly as possible to the Rhine River, and capture any available bridges in the vicin-

Generals Jacob Allen, George Patton, Alexander Patch, and Omar Bradley confer in March, 1945.

ity of Worms. The next few days, filled with rapid movement and little or no rest, tested the endurance of the Hellcats.

The advance westward across Germany began on the morning of
March 18, with all three combat commands moving forward against
light opposition. Making steady progress, the Hellcats captured
three hundred prisoners of war, two 105-millimeter howitzers, and
numerous horses used by the Germans to pull their cannons.
Continuing the American blitzkrieg the following day, the 12th was
slowed down only by the large numbers of German soldiers surrendering. The Hellcats captured some 2,500 Germans, as well as tons of
enemy supplies and equipment. Slashing through light enemy
defenses, on March 20 the Hellcats destroyed a railroad train and
captured twenty-five enemy trucks, continually moving to the
southeast towards the Rhine River.

Hellcats taking a breather during the race to the Rhine River.

The 56th Armored Infantry Battalion won the race to the Rhine, reaching it just before midnight on March 20. The 17th Armored Infantry Battalion and the 23rd Tank Battalion of Combat Command R reached the Rhine shortly after midnight, and elements of the division turned south along the Rhine, sending combat patrols into Ludwigshaffen, then continuing on south, still searching for a usable bridge.

German resistance increased as the Hellcat Division pushed through one riverside town after another, and the rate of advance slowed. Whenever particularly strong opposition was encountered, the Hellcats called in air support, and watched as P-47 fighter-bombers wreaked their devastation on the enemy. Combat Command B and the 92nd Cavalry Reconnaissance Squadron fought their way into Speyer on March 23, but the Germans blew up the coveted bridge before the Hellcats could seize it. So the quest continued, moving ever southward along the west bank of the Rhine. On March 24 Combat Command R entered Germersheim, where the bridges were once again destroyed, and made contact with the 14th

Gen. Devers decorating Gen. de Lattre.

Armored Division moving up from the south. The race to the Rhine River was over. At noon on March 24 the 12th Armored Division reverted to control of the XXI Corps of the Seventh Army.

The Hellcats did not capture an intact bridge across the Rhine, but in all other respects the division performed admirably and covered itself with glory. One unit, Troop D of the 92nd Cavalry Reconnaissance Squadron, was singled out for a particular honor, the Presidential Unit Citation. Troop D spearheaded the division's advance from Trier to the Rhine, a distance of seventy-two miles, fighting four separate engagements and disrupting large enemy formations. Troop D captured over one thousand prisoners of war, eighteen anti-tank guns, fourteen other artillery pieces, dozens of motor vehicles, and hundreds of horse-drawn vehicles, all in a space of seven days .[104]

The lightning thrust across the German Rhineland was a model of mobile warfare, and showed what a well-equipped, well-trained, and seasoned armored division could accomplish. The 12th Armored Division was approaching its peak of perfection.

"I wish to express commendation and appreciation for the spirit, aggressiveness, and valor with which the 12th Armored Division so successfully performed its every combat mission while operationally attached to this headquarters from March 31, 1945, to May 5, 1945."

Major General F. W. Milburn, XXI Corps Commander.

CHAPTER 7

Central Germany and Landsberg

Returning to the Seventh Army fold on March 24, the Hellcats spent a few days enjoying a well-earned rest. Many went on "reconnaissance patrols" and in nearby houses found cellars full of wine and champagne, which they naturally had to sample. After an all-too-brief respite from the war, the Hellcats once more went on the offensive. Shortly after midnight on March 28 the division began crossing a pontoon bridge across the Rhine at Worms.

After passing through the U.S. 3rd Infantry Division on the east side of the Rhine, the 12th Armored Division again became an armored spearhead, this time for the Seventh Army. The Hellcats received the assignment of blazing a trail across Bavaria, and seizing a crossing of the Main River in the vicinity of Wurzburg. Combat Commands A and B moved out abreast, while Combat Command R was in division reserve, and the 92nd Cavalry Reconnaissance Squadron once again led the charge.

Initial enemy resistance was light, and the division made good progress moving east. As the Hellcats penetrated farther into

The Hellcats crossed the Rhine River at Worms on March 28, 1945.

Germany, however, they began encountering stiffer pockets of resistance. Whenever that happened, the lead units would pull back and let the armored field artillery soften up the impediments. Then the race would begin once more. As the combat patrols neared Wurzburg, the Hellcats could see the P-47 fighter-bombers unloading on the German city. American planes were not the only ones in the air, however, as elements of the 12th found themselves on the receiving end of enemy strafing and bombing missions. On April 2 the 572nd Anti-Aircraft Artillery Battalion claimed two enemy planes shot down and two more damaged.[105]

During this phase of the fighting, when the Combat Commands of the division were probing enemy defenses and exploiting weak spots, the British Broadcasting Company made the following announcement on a radio program: "The U.S. Seventh Army's 12th Armored Division, near Wurzburg, is the farthest Allied unit into Germany at this time." After being the unnamed "Mystery Division" during the Third Army drive, a little recognition was music to the ears of the exhausted but triumphant Hellcats.

The 119th Engineers built this Bailey bridge over the Main River at Wurzburg.

Hellcats entering one of many towns in their blitz across central Germany.

The fighting efficiency of the task forces and combat commands of the division continually improved as the Hellcats gained experience as well as updated equipment. Armored task forces, smaller than combat commands, became the lead elements of the division

The Hellcats captured thousands of German prisoners during the last weeks of the war.

and came to be organized in the following fashion. Leading off would be a platoon of four or five tanks, followed by a company of infantry in halftracks. Next in line was the remainder of the tank company, followed by another company of armored infantry. Following that was a platoon of engineers, then a medical detachment, then an anti-aircraft detail, and finally the headquarters company with its assault guns and mortars. The task force commander most often was found in a jeep near the head of the column.

By this time in the war all the kinks had been worked out of the communications system, and the division finally had plenty of radios. A constant chatter between units, and between the battalion commander and his subordinates, kept everyone working together and knowledgeable about the positions and

> It was snowing miserably, and we were wet and chilled to the marrow. Soon after we took position, whole columns of Krauts, mounted and dismounted, some armed, some unarmed, began marching and riding into Pfraumdorf, apparently desirous of being taken prisoner.
>
> Lieutenant Clinton E. Seitz
> 495th Armored Field Artillery
> Battalion

problems of the various units. Some pundits criticized the U.S. Army for relying upon and using radios too much during the war, but good

More German prisoners being brought into detention centers.

Pausing before an attack on the next German town.

Hellcats speeding through Dinkelsbuhl, Germany.

communications keeps everyone working together as a team. Good communications meant that the tanks could speak with the infantry, and both units with the artillery spotters flying overhead, so artillery fire could be brought to bear almost instantly.[106] The abundant communications of April 1945 was a far cry from the almost total lack of communications during the disastrous battles at Herrlisheim in January.

Operations of the combat elements began to display similar characteristics. The armored task force columns would move out toward their assigned objectives, always on the alert for roadblocks, ambushes, or centers of resistance. When the enemy was encountered, the infantry would bail out of their halftracks and move into the attack. If the resistance was particularly strong, then tanks and artillery were brought up to deal with the problem. If air support was required, each combat command had an attached air liaison officer who was a member of the Army Air Forces. He would get on the radio to his buddies in the Tactical Air Force units assigned to the Seventh Army, and soon fighter-bombers would appear overhead to pulverize the enemy. In short, the 12th Armored Division, as a part of a larg-

A German general captured by soldiers of the 12th Armored Division.

Street fighting in Coberg, Germany.

Hellcat tanks fighting through Erback, Germany.

er military force, had become a well-oiled, terribly efficient killing machine.

On April 3 elements of the 222nd Infantry Regiment, originally part of the 42nd Infantry Division but temporarily attached to Combat Command A, crossed the Main River in assault boats and secured a bridgehead on the east bank of the river in the town of Wurzburg. The 12th Armored Division's 119th Engineers moved up and began construction of a Bailey bridge. Other elements of the division seized their assigned objectives in the area, then consolidated their positions.[107]

On April 5 Combat Command A began moving through the city of Wurzburg. Rain and poor visibility added to the danger inherent in urban warfare, and enemy mortar and anti-tank fire slowed the progress. After passing through Wurzburg, Combat Command A, attached to the 42nd Infantry Division, began moving to the northeast toward Schweinfurt, an important industri-

> *The young soldier's breath was labored. Cold perspiration stood out on his gray skin. He looked at me with agony in his eyes and spoke to me and said in words that I will never forget so long as I live, 'Major, I appreciate what you are doing and telling me, but I am dying. I have a little baby son whom I have not seen. He's only two weeks old. Now he will never know me and never get to know me. I am sorry. I am very sorry for that.'*
>
> Major F. W. Carstens
> 493rd Armored Field Artillery Battalion

493rd AFA passing through Erback, Germany.

Soldiers of Co. D, 43rd Tank Bn, guarding the Dillingen Bridge.

al area.[108] Many American bombers and their crews had been lost while attacking the ball-bearing manufacturing plants in Schweinfurt. The city eventually fell to infantrymen carrying rifles and machineguns, supported by tanks and artillery.

General Allen greeting troops from India liberated by the Hellcats.

Meanwhile, the remainder of the division began a heavy recon-naissance-in-force in the areas adjacent to the Main River. Numerous small towns were captured or occupied, but in a few oth-ers resistance was so strong that reconnaissance units had to pull back out of range of heavy small arms fire and panzerfaust anti-tank weapons. Heavier armored units then came up and dealt with the troublemakers.

While waiting for their next major assignment, the Hellcats learned of the death of their president, Franklin Delano Roosevelt. With his twelve years in office, President Roosevelt was the only chief executive most of the younger Hellcats could remember. Many of the men wondered what would become of their country and the war effort with President Roosevelt gone, but they had little time to pause and reflect.

On April 13 the division received its orders: advance in the direc-tion of Nurnburg and points south. Once again the armored columns filled the roads and byways, and the Hellcats moved out. Capturing sometimes dozens of small towns each day, the Hellcats were greeted by white flags in one town and machinegun fire in the next. Although moving rapidly through southern Germany, Hellcats were wounded and killed each day they advanced. Fighting in the

Allied POWs cheering their 12th Armored liberators.

towns was especially nerve-wracking, as determined enemy soldiers could hide in the rubble of destroyed buildings, or in the upper floors of taller buildings that the Hellcat artillery had spared. Blown-up bridges and well-defended road blocks also added to the danger and death toll, chipping away at the manpower of the division.

New orders reached the division on April 17, telling the Hellcats to turn south and advance on Munich. At daybreak on the following morning the Hellcats began cutting a swath toward Munich, the Danube River, and points south. Hundreds of prisoners were captured each day, as well as mountains of supplies and equipment. Combat Command A even captured forty enemy combat planes on the ground.

As the division neared the Danube, the Hellcats made a concerted effort to capture a bridge intact. A task force composed of the 66th Armored Infantry Battalion and companies from the 43rd Tank Battalion advanced rapidly to Dillingen, and just before noon on April 22 the task force shot its way into the center of town and found a bridge that had not yet been blown. As the tanks took up covering positions on the near side of the river, a squad of 66th doughboys raced across the bridge, capturing a group of German demolitions men who were preparing to destroy it. After securing a small bridge-head on the far side, the Hellcats conducted a quick search and dis-

Entrance to Hurlack Camp, one of the prisons liberated by the 12th Armored near Landsberg.

Hellcats investigating the horrors of one of the Landsberg camps.

covered six 500-pound aircraft bombs under the bridge, wired in place to blow up the crossing. Engineers deactivated the bomb, and Combat Command A crossed the Danube and continued moving south. Securing the two lane concrete bridge was a significant

Soldiers of the 12th were stunned by the sights of the Landsberg prison camps.

achievement for the Hellcat Division and hastened the occupation of southern Germany.[109]

The Germans did not take lightly the seizure of a major crossing over the Danube River, and the German Luftwaffe made several attempts to bomb the bridge. The 572nd Anti-Aircraft Artillery Battalion, dug in to protect the bridge, shot down six enemy planes on April 23 and another three on the following day.[110]

The next major stop on the Hellcat Express was the city of Landsberg, on the Lech River. On the way south, the 92nd Cavalry Reconnaissance Squadron and other elements of Combat Command R captured an airfield near Hiltengen on the Wertach River on April 26. There they found more than forty ME-262 fighter jets, of which twenty were still in working order.

Combat Command A continued moving south and late in the day of the 26th crossed the Lech River, with some of the tanks and half-tracks bumping their way along the crossties of a railway bridge, while others crossed a 240-foot long temporary bridge installed by the 119th Engineers. After crossing the river, Combat Command A cleared six towns and captured many enemy soldiers, while liberating 2,800 Allied prisoners, including 1,400 U.S. troops. The division continued to advance against scattered resistance on the 27th and during that day alone captured 5,200 prisoners of war, two hospitals with 1,300 patients, and an airfield with more than sixty airplanes.[111]

One of the most disturbing scenes of the war awaited the Hellcats at the small German city of Landsberg am Lech, better known simply as Landsberg. Interestingly enough, a young Adolph Hitler had been held in a prison in Landsberg in 1923 for attempting to overthrow the German government. While languishing in his prison cell, he wrote his autobiography, *Mein Kampf,* or *My Struggle.*

During World War II Landsberg was a sub-camp of the huge concentration camp complex at Dachau. When the Hellcats rolled into the area on April 27, some of the soldiers observed what appeared to be barracks behind prison-type fences, so they went over to investigate, thinking there might be American or Allied prisoners of war being held there. What they found shocked the most hardened of the combat soldiers.

In a series of eleven separate camps in the vicinity of Landsberg, forty to fifty thousand Jews and other political prisoners were incarcerated, where they had been starved, beaten, and mistreated in unimaginable ways. Many hundreds of the inmates were murdered by the German SS guards just before the Americans arrived to liberate the camps. If the Hellcats had not captured the Dillingen Bridge, and thus overrun the camps before the SS guards could act, the Nazi guards would have killed all of the concentration camp inmates. By their prompt action, the Hellcats saved tens of thousands of lives.[112]

April was a busy month for the 12th Armored Division, as the Hellcats captured more than 30,000 enemy soldiers. The great achievements during the month were not without cost, as 234 Hellcats were killed or missing in action during the month, including two men in one of the artillery spotter planes, and an additional 723 officers and men were wounded in action. The deaths of these men was especially disheartening, as everyone could see that German resistance was crumbling and the final victory over the German enemy was just a matter of time.[113]

"A representative of the German High Command signed the unconditional surrender of all German land, sea, and air forces in Europe to the Allied Expeditionary Force and simultaneously to the Soviet High Command at zero one four one hours Central European Time, seven May under which all forces will cease active operations at zero zero zero one Baker hours nine May. Effective immediately all offensive operations by Allied Expeditionary Force will cease and troops will remain in present positions."

General Dwight D. Eisenhower, Commander
Supreme Headquarters Allied Expeditionary Force

CHAPTER 8

The End of the War and Home

By the end of April and the beginning of May, the German enemy was very nearly defeated. While pockets of German resistance could engage in temporary delaying actions, the disintegrating German Army could not mount any type of credible defense. The German war machine was broken and could not be repaired. But even though the end of the war was at hand, the fighting continued. Many of the Hellcats became more cautious, though, as no one wanted to be the last casualty of the war.

The division received orders to continue attacking to the southeast, cross into Austria, and block the Brenner Pass leading from the Austrian Alps into Italy. Snow drifts became more common in the steep, mountainous country, and the roads were narrow and winding. The task forces progressed as best they could, generally making good time, but meeting some resistance from small bands of the fanatical SS soldiers who refused to accept the inevitable German defeat.

On May 2 the 17th Armored Infantry Battalion and a platoon of tanks from Company C, 23rd Tank Battalion, set a ground force record for movement through enemy territory. In seven hours the task force covered sixty miles traveling two vehicles abreast down the German autobahn, or freeway. After halting for the evening, the lead Hellcats discovered

German children watch as American armor comes into town.

that SS engineers had destroyed a bridge after the task force passed over it, isolating the small group from the remainder of Combat Command R. Once the bulk of the combat command found an alternate route and caught up with the advance elements, the 23rd Tank Battalion led the procession across the Austrian border on the afternoon of May 3.

While Combat Command R continued its advance on Innsbruck, Austria, the remainder of the division consolidated the areas they occupied. On May 3 the division made its largest capture of enemy personnel, netting 12,060 prisoners of war. On the following day Combat Command R, advancing against stiff resistance, was relieved in position by the 36th Infantry Division. Many of the Hellcats renewed acquaintances with the "T-patchers," so-called because of the "T-for-Texas" patch they wore on their uniforms. The 36th Division had previously relieved the Hellcats at Herrlisheim, after the bloody battle in January.

Hellcats eat a hurried meal during the race to Austria.

The 12th Armored Division became Seventh Army reserve on May 4 and moved back out of the front lines. That meant that, barring any unforeseen circumstances, the fighting for the Hellcats was over. The division began moving back into Germany to take up occupation duties in the vicinity of Heidenheim. Then on May 6 the Hellcats received the word for which they had been waiting so long: the German Army group in southern Germany had surrendered. The fighting was over for the 12th Armored Division.[114]

Once the Hellcats assembled in their occupation areas, a garrison peacetime routine prevailed. The men had the opportunity to clean up and take hot showers, have good hot meals in the mess halls, and shop in the Post Exchange. USO shows came to entertain the soldiers, and passes were readily available, so many of the Hellcats visited Paris, the French Riviera, and England. The stress of combat was over, and it was time to unwind, relax, and enjoy life. Germany officially surrendered to the allies on May 8, and a great sigh of relief was heard throughout Europe.

During the course of its five months in combat, the 12th Armored Division had transformed from a green, inexperienced collection of individuals into an efficient, well-organized, veteran combat division, respected by friend and foe alike. During the thirty-seven day

17th Armored Infantrymen riding tanks into Innsbruck, Austria.

lightning thrust from the Rhine River to Austria, the division captured 70,166 enemy prisoners of war, and liberated 8,500 Allied prisoners of war and approximately 50,000 non-military prisoners. Among the civilian prisoners freed by the Hellcats were former French premiers Eduard Daladier and Paul Reynaud, two former commanders of the French armies, the son of World War I French statesman Georges Clemenceau, and the sister of Charles De Gaulle.[115] During the course of their efforts to liberate France, the Hellcats paid a price. The division suffered 2,647 men wounded or injured in action and had 351 men captured by the enemy and made prisoners of war The highest price was paid by 870 young American men who lost their lives while serving their country overseas.[116]

With the conclusion of hostilities in Europe, thoughts of the men naturally turned to going home. The Army came up with a system to send individual soldiers back to the states based on accumulated points. A soldier received points for time in service, time in combat, wounds, medals awarded, and other factors. So everyone began trying to figure out how many points he had. And with the point system

Heidenheim, Germany was the headquarters of the 12th Armored Division occupation zone.

The end of hostilities meant more hot chow, always appreciated by soldiers.

The end of the war meant more trips to rest areas, where Red Cross Girls entertained the soldiers.

The USO brought people like Jack Benny to entertain the troops.

Hellcats play football to pass the time during occupation duty.

Camp Lucky Strike near Marseilles, France was the last European stop for many Hellcats.

in place, many Hellcat veterans began leaving the division and going home. Low-point men, often replacement troops who had only recently joined the division, faced the prospect of going to the Pacific Theater of Operations and fighting the Japanese.

During May and June the Hellcats continued with their occupation duties, safeguarding strategic areas and processing German

One of the many ships that carried the victorious Hellcats home at last.

prisoners. In July the division began losing its identity, as thousands of low-point Hellcats transferred to other units, and high-point men from other divisions joined the Hellcats for the trip back to the states. In late July General Allen left the division to take over as commander of the 1st Armored Division, and Brigadier General Willard Holbrook of the 11th Armored Division became the Hellcats' new commanding officer.

In November the remaining Hellcats received word that they were finally headed home. After a long trip to Marseilles, France, the soldiers of the 12th boarded ships for one last voyage, one without the worry of German U-boats, a trip that would take them back to their families and loved ones. Upon arrival at Camp Kilmer, New Jersey, the headquarters section turned in the division's battle flags, and the 12th Armored Division of the United States Army was officially deactivated. The Hellcat Division had passed into history.[117]

EPILOGUE

After the conclusion of hostilities in Europe but before the 12th Armored Division sailed for home, members of the division had time to think about what they had done during the course of the war, and to appreciate the bonds of friendship that the men developed during their time together. Everyone knew the war was over, and all the men would soon be going their separate ways. But the Hellcats did not want to lose the feelings of comradeship, of brotherhood, that time spent together in the most trying of circumstances had promoted.

On September 15, 1945, the division's third anniversary, the soldiers formed the 12th Armored Division Association. The officers of the association scheduled a reunion for all members of the division, and that first reunion was held at the Hotel Commodore in New York City on September 13-14, 1947. Since that time the 12th Armored Division Association has continued to hold annual reunions, while also publishing a monthly newsletter. Over the years many of the Hellcat veterans scheduled their annual holidays around the divisional reunions, and children and grandchildren of the Hellcats have grown up attending the 12th Armored Division Association reunions.

During the 1990s Dr. Vernon Williams, a history professor at Abilene Christian University, began attending reunions to collect oral histories from the veterans of the 12th. Then in 1994 the officers of the association decided to retire their archives to the Abilene Christian University Library. When word went out to the veterans that they could send their personal collections of war memorabilia to Abilene, the university library was overwhelmed with the amount of material received. So in 1999 a group of 12th Armored Division Association members and concerned citizens from Abilene formed the 12th Armored Division Memorial Museum Foundation. That same year the board of directors of the foundation purchased a building for a museum in Abilene.

After more than two years of fund-raising, building remodeling, and exhibit design and construction, the board of directors opened the museum during the annual reunion of the 12th Armored Division Association on October 6, 2001. The 12th Armored Division Memorial Museum, located at 1289 North Second Street in Abilene, Texas, is the only museum in the United States dedicated to preserving the memory of a World War II armored division.

APPENDIX A

12th Armored Division Chronology

1942

July—General Staff Corps officers selected for the division began training at Command and General Staff School, Fort Leavenworth, Kansas.

August 17—First formal guard mount at Camp Campbell, Kentucky.

September 15—12th Armored Division formally activated at Camp Campbell, Kentucky.

October 24—Filler replacements began to arrive.

November 10—Mobilization Training Program started.

1943

February 1—Nickname "Hellcats" formally adopted.

April 1—56th Armored Infantry Regiment and attached personnel guarded route of President Roosevelt who was traveling in Tennessee.

April 27—First overnight division exercise.

July 16-17—Participated in IV Armored Corps two-day problem.

September 6 to November 1—Tennessee Maneuvers.

November—Division reorganized to "light" armored division structure with battalions rather than regiments.

November 20—Arrived at Camp Barkeley near Abilene, Texas.

1944

January 1 and 2—12th Armored Division Rodeo at Abilene Fair Grounds.

March 8—44th Tank Battalion detached and sent to Pacific Theater. 714th Tank Battalion returned to 12th Armored Division.

July 7—Army Ground Forces test at Camp Bowie.

August 8—Movement orders for the division arrived from Washington.

August 15—Division Review to honor Major General Carlos Brewer.

August 16—Major General Brewer relieved, Major General Douglass T. Greene assumed command of the division.

September 8—First units of the division arrive at Camp Shanks, New York.

September 17—General Greene relieved, ordered to Washington.

September 19—Major General Roderick R. Allen assumed command of the division; last train of the division departed for the Port of Embarkation.

September 20—Division departed the United States.

October 2—Arrived in England.

November 9—Departed England

November 11—Division begins landing in France

November 17—Major portion of division in bivouac at Auffey, France.

November 25—Hellcats captured their first German prisoners.

November 27—12th Armored Division assigned to 6th Army Group, Lieutenant Jacob L. Devers, commanding.

November 28—12th Armored Division assigned to Seventh Army, Lieutenant General Alexander M. Patch, commanding. Advance party left Auffey to arrange billets in vicinity of Luneville.

November 29—First elements of the division departed Auffey for a new location near Lunneville, near Soissons.

December 1—Division Command Post opened in Luneville.

December 2—Division closed in assembly area in the vicinity of Luneville.

December 4—572nd Anti-Aircraft Artillery Automatic Weapons Battalion (Self-propelled) attached to the division.

December 5—Division assigned to XV Corps, Major General Wade Haislip, commanding. Number 2 gun section, Battery A, 493rd Armored Field Artillery, temporarily attached to 44th Infantry Division, fired the division's first shot in combat.

December 7—Division Command Post opened at Domfessel.

December 8—Relief of 4th Armored Division completed by 0600.

December 9—First ground attack, launched by Combat Command A against the Maginot Line, commenced at 0400. Singling captured at 0445. Second objective, high ground beyond Singling, taken 0458. Binning village and half of Binning Barracks taken.

December 10—Rohrbach captured at 0830.

December 12—Guising and Bettwiller (Division objective) occupied.

December 13—Division Command Post opened Rahling.

December 15—Elements of 25th Cavalry Reconnaissance Squadron relieved elements of the 92nd Cavalry from screen across the Division front.

December 16—Division Command Post opened at Rimsdorf .

December 17—Relief of Division by elements 80th Infantry Division begun.

December 18—Relief by 80th Infantry Division completed.

December 19—25th Cavalry Recon Squadron (4th Armored Division) and forward elements, 80th Infantry Division relieved by 92nd Cavalry Reconnaissance Squadron. Counter Reconnaissance screen established across Division front and contact with the 87th Infantry Division on the left and the 44th Infantry Division on the right established.

December 20—Remainder of the Division moved to forward assembly areas.

December 21—Combat Command B began attack at 0415. 56th Armored Infantry Battalion occupied Utweiler at 1830, the first German town captured by the 12th Armored Division.

December 25—After being relieved by the 100th Infantry Division, the 12th went to corps reserve for maintenance and rehabilitation.

December 26—Division moved from forward assembly areas to XV Corps reserve. Division Command Post located at Albestroff.

27 December 27—Division relieved from XV Corps, assigned to XXI Corps.

29 December 29—Division Command Post opened at Dieuze. Division assembled in the vicinity of Dieuze. All units continued maintenance, reorganization and rehabilitation.

1945

January 6—Division released from XXI Corps and attached to VI Corps, Major General Edward H. Brooks, commanding. Division began movement to assembly area near Hochfelden prior to renewed offensive action.

January 7—Combat Command B (56th Armored Infantry Battalion, 714th Tank Battalion, elements of 119th Armored Engineer Battalion, and division artillery) attached to 79th Infantry Division.

January 8—Division Command Post opened at Hochfelden. Division closed in bivouac in the vicinity of Hoehfelden. Combat Command B commenced attack on Herrlisheim.

January 9—Counter Reconnaissance screen around Corps south flank established by 92nd Cavalry Reconnaissance Squadron. Defensive road blocks, mine fields, demolitions put in by 119th Armored Engineer Battalion around the Corps south boundary.

January 13— Remainder of Division ordered to attack through elements 79th Infantry Division to destroy enemy forces west of Rhine River in the Offendorf-Herrlisheim-Drusenheim area.

January 15— 1945 Division Command Post moved to Brumath.

January 16-19—Battle of Herrlisheim and Steinwald Woods.

January 16—Combat Command A moved to assembly area, prepared to seize Steinwald Woods and attack Offendorf. Combat Command B ordered to attack at 0300. Combat Command A crossed canal at 0520 and was stopped 300 yards west of woods by heavy enemy small arms, mortar and artillery fire. Combat Command B attack held up by heavy small arms, and artillery fire, withdrew to Rohrwiller for reorganization.

January 17—Combat Command A attacked 0714, entered town of Herrlisheim. By 0849 17th Armored Infantry Battalion occupied one-third of south part of town. 43rd Tank Battalion overran numerous enemy positions, but was stopped around Herrlisheim-

Gnmbsheim railroad track by heavy 88mm and 75mm anti-tank fire. 66th Armored Infantry Battalion repulsed by heavy fire from edge of Steinwald Woods. Combat Command B attack held up by bridge destroyed by enemy fire so heavy as to prevent engineers from building. Supported Combat Command A by fire. 43rd Tank Battalion entered east edge Herrlisheim finder heavy fire.

January 18—Enemy counter-attack of 200 men and 6 to 8 tanks repulsed. Second enemy counter-attack by 300 men supported by tanks surrounded and captured or destroyed major elements of the 17th Armored Infantry Battalion and 43rd Tank Battalion. No further contact with these troops was possible. Enemy counter-attacked constantly throughout afternoon and evening, supported by tanks and heavy artillery, mortar and small arms fire, against elements of Combat Command A and Combat Command B, which withdrew to defensive positions along the canal.

January 19—Enemy counter-attacks broken up by artillery and close-support bombing and strafing missions. Defensive positions maintained in the face of constant small enemy infantry and armored counter-attacks. Combat Command A halted, with heavy enemy losses, a flanking counter-attack by a German force estimated at 800 Infantry and 50 tanks at 1600.

January 20—Division relieved by elements of the 36th Infantry Division beginning at 0230. Tanks temporarily remained in support of 36th Infantry Division. Division moved to assembly area vicinity, Hochielden.

January 22—Division came under the control of the First French Army, began maintenance, rehabilitation, and reorganization.

January 26-February 5—Division assisted in clearing the Colmar Pocket area of France.

January 26—Division Command Post opened Ittenheim. Division closed in assembly area, vicinity Ittenheim. Prepared to repel possible counter-attack from vicinity Hoerdt and Kilstett. Division Artillery in position to support the French 3rd Algerian Infantry Division.

February 3—Division Command Post opened in Zollenberg at 0430. Combat Command B attacked south from Colmar at 0930, meeting heavy mortar and small arms fire. Remainder of Division closed in vicinity Selestat at on February 4, coming under the control of the U.S. XXI Corps. Combat Command B continued attack to seize Sundheften and St. Croix.

February 4—Division Command Post opened at Colmar. Combat Command B and Combat Command R attacked to the south abreast, with Combat Command B on the left continuing the attack to seize Sundheffen and St. Croix, and upon relief aid by elements of the 109th Infantry Regiment exploit to the south. Combat Command R relieved French elements in zone exploiting to the south and taking Herrlisheim-pres-Colmar.

February 5—Infantry elements of Combat Command A entered Rouffaeh at 0512 and other elements of Combat Command A moved around the town, sealing off exits and meeting French forces which had reached the south edge of town during the night. Guebersehwir and Pfaffenheim were cleared of the enemy at 0835. Anti-tank fire defending road blocks and heavy mortar fire were met by the Division during this period, particularly in the vicinity just south of Colmar.

February 7—Division ordered to block the passes leading east from the Vosges Mountains.

February 9—Major General Milburn, commanding XXI Corps, awarded Bronze Star to Maj. Gen. Allen for his part of the action in the Colmar pocket

February 10—Division received commendation from Lieutenant General Jacob L. Devers, Commanding General, 6th Army Group and from General de Goislard de Monsabert, the Commanding General of the French 3rd Algerian Infantry Division. Division relieved elements of the 10th Armored Division in a counter-reconnaissance Screen south of the Maginot Line and east and west of the Sarre River.

February 11—Division Command Post opened at Faulquemont and Division passed to control of XV Corps upon closing in the vicinity of Faulquemont.

February 28—Division passed to control XXI Corps.

March 2—Combat Command A ordered to support attack of 70th Infantry Division by occupying and defending Forbach and Stiring Wendel when cleared by elements of 70th Infantry Division.

March 3—Combat Command A occupied Forbach.

March 5—Task Force 1, Combat Comd A, occupied Stiring Wendel.

March 15—92nd Cavalry Reconnaissance Squadron, attached to 63rd Infantry Division closed, vicinity St. Avold.

March 17—Division commenced move at 0700 to assembly area, vicinity Apache, attached to XX Corps, Third Army (General Patton), upon arrival.

March 17 to March 24— Combat Command A cleared and occupied Ludwigshaven, Combat Command B seized and cleared Speyer. Combat Command R occupied Westheim and Nieder Lustadt and attacked and cleared Germersheim..

March 24—Division reverted to control of XXI Corps and Seventh Army.

March 26—Combat Command A relieved by 100th Infantry Division, Combat Command B relieved by 71st Infantry Division, Combat Command R relieved by elements of the 71st Infantry Division, 14th Armored Division and 36th Infantry Division. 12th Armored Division assembled in the vicinity of Deidesheim, passing to control XV Corps.

March 27—Division commenced movement to cross bridge in the vicinity of Worms.

March 28—Division closed vicinity Lorsch and began advance to the east passing through elements of the 3rd Infantry Division.

March 29—Division Command Post closed vicinity Beerfelden. Combat Command A and Combat Command B attacked abreast, followed by Combat Command R in the face of moderate resistance.

March 31—Combat Command A encountered stiff resistance at Wortheim. Bypassed city and continued attack on Wurzburg. Combat Command B advanced along assigned routes, meeting moderate resistance. Combat Command R attacked in two columns and captured Boxberg in spite of heavy rocket and small arms fire. Division passed to control of XXI Corps.

April 1—Combat Command A captured Hettstadt. Enemy counter-attack repulsed, town secured at 1600A. Combat Command B seized Rottenbauer at 1200 and Oehsenfurt at 1330. Combat Command R took Schweigern, Sachsczfleur and Edelfinger.

April 3—Town of Marienburg occupied by 0418. Elements of Combat Command A crossed the Main River in assault boats and established a bridgehead on the east bank in the town of Wurzburg. Combat Command B elements crossed the Main River in the vicinity of Ochsenfurt, advancing north against prepared positions stubbornly defended.

April 4—Light elements of Combat Command A crossed the Main River to aid infantry elements, 42nd Infantry Division, in clearing Wurzburg. Combat Command B occupied Erlach. Combat Command R cleared and occupied Herrnberehtheim and Gnotzheim.

April 5—Enemy counter-attack in Wurzburg repulsed. Combat Command A moved north toward Sehweinfurt, taking Rottendorf. Combat Command B seized Kitzingen, crossed a damaged bridge and established a bridgehead on the east bank of the Main River. Westheim, Theilheim, Beibereid and Reppernorf cleared on west side of river to protect combat command's left flank and rear. Combat Command R cleared Bullenheim, Wassendorf, Iffigheim and Seinsheim.

April 6—Combat Command B advanced south from Kitzingen bridgehead and captured towns of Marktbreit, Obernbreit, Tiefensteckheim. Light resistance encountered. Combat Command B cleared Willanzheim, Herrnsheim, Huttenheim, Herrlsheim, Menehsendheim. Combat command objective Einersheim taken.

April 7—101st Cavalry Reconnaissance Group attached to 12th Armored Division. Combat Command A cleared Bergtheim, Opferbach, Esselben, Waigelsheim against stiff resistance. Combat Command A attached to 42nd Infantry Division. Remainder of the Division assembled for maintenance and rehabilitation

April 8—101st Cavalry Reconnaissance Group and 92nd Cavalry Reconnaissance Squadron were given the mission of initiating reconnaissance in Corps zone. Cavalry advanced slowly against stiff resistance. Blown bridges and well-defended road blocks delayed advance of Combat Command B. Combat Command R moved to destroy enemy in zone meeting strong enemy fire, mines and demolitions.

April 9—Combat Command B took Stadt Schwarzachheidt and Klein Langheim with heavy resistance by hostile tanks and strong artillery fire. Combat Command R cleared lleusch, Weigenheim and Geekenheim against stiff resistance. Division Command Post opened at the Kitzingen airfield.

April 11—Combat Command B attacked south and southeast, clearing Castell, Greuth, Stierhofstetten, Ober Schenfeld, Ziegenbaeh, Marktbibart and Altamannshousen. Combat Command R attacked southeast against light resistance, taking Pfaffenhoffen, Ober Scheckenbach, Uffenheim, Uttenheffen, Neuherberg and Ohrenbaeh.

April 12—Combat Command A cleared Krautestheim, Markt Nerdheim, Neundorf, Ingelstadt and Ezellleim. Combat Command R completed encirclement of enemy by establishing contact with 116th Cavalry Reconnaissance Squadron (101st Cavalry Reconnaissance Group) at Aub and with 12th Infantry Regiment (4th Infantry Division) at Waldmannshoffen. Langensteinach, Wellmarsbach, Simmershoffen, Equarhoffen and Auernhoffen were cleared. Six anti-tank guns, twelve tanks, three 155-mm guns and two ME109s were destroyed. 508 prisoners of war taken.

April 13—Combat Command A reverted to Division control. Combat Command B occupied nine towns against little resistance. Combat Command R mopped up woods and scattered enemy groups vicinity of Aub and Uffenheim. l0lst Cavalry Group continued reconnaissance in assigned zone, meeting stiff resistance.

April 14—Combat Command A relieved by elements 42nd Infantry Division at 0700. March to assembly area in the vicinity of Ullstadt. Combat Command B attacked at 1130, advanced to Aisch River, over which all bridges had been destroyed. A temporary bridge was completed at 1830 and armored elements crossed establishing a bridgehead. Main resistance passive defense. Combat Command R commenced attack at 1145A on Aris-Ob Dasehstetten, Azebach. Division Command Post opened at Uffenheim at 1430.

April 15—Division continued advance to the east. Road blocks strongly defended by small arms, anti-tank, rocket, mortar and artillery fire. Six enemy tanks captured or destroyed.

April 16—Combat Command A captured a bridge intact at Langengenn, occupying the town at 1600. Combat Command B advanced to Zohn River over which bridges were found to be blown. Division Command Post opened Illesheim at 1645.

April 18—Combat Command A moved into position to cut southern escape route from Nurnberg. Combat Command B advanced from Heilsbrenn to Ansbach, destroyed ten 88-mm anti-tank guns and one 150-mm howitzer. Entered Ansbach from north and northeast. Combat Command R cleared enemy from sixteen towns between Rugland and Ansbach. Division Command Post opened at 1735in the vicinity of Ob Sachstetten.

April 19—Combat Command A occupied Schwabach and Buchschwabach, capturing 250 prisoners of war, 40 enemy combat planes on the ground and an ammunition dump. Combat Command B and Combat Command R cleared Ansbach.

 April 20—Combat Command A captured Mayersbrenn, Schopfloeh, Lescugutingen and Dinkelsbuhl before advance was halted by a blown bridge. Combat Command B entered Feuchtwangen at 1005. Combat Command R attacked Feuchtwangen in conjunction with Combat Command B, then turned west and occupied Reichenbach. Estimated 1280 PW's taken, 40 combat aircraft captured or destroyed on the ground.

April 21—Combat Command A cleared thirteen towns. Remainder of Division assembled prior to attack to seize Danube crossings. Estimated 1100 prisoners taken during period.

April 22—One Task Force reached Lauingen to find bridge over Danube River blown as they entered town. Task Force 2 captured a bridge at Dillingen. One infantry company crossed and Task Force 1 moved from Lauingen to Dillingen, crossed the bridge to reinforce Task Force 2 bridgehead. Task Force 1 attacked and captured Fristingen. Combat Command B captured Hochstadt. Bridge blown as troops approached town. Combat Command R mopping up bypassed centers of resistance. Estimated 750 prisoners captured.

April 23—Combat Command A secured Helzheim and Kieklingen. Estimated 2650 prisoners taken.

April 24—15th Regimental Combat Team (3rd Infantry Division) attached to Combat Command A upon arrival in bridgehead area. Wertingen resisting strong attack of Task Force 1, Combat Command A and First Battalion, 15th RCT. 2,020 prisoners, ten planes, thirty 88-mm, multiple anti-aircraft guns, one 75mm howitzer and two military hospitals captured.

April 25—First Battalion, 15th Regimental Combat Team seized Wertingen at 1030. 15th RCT relieved from attachment effective 1830. Combat Command B advanced southwest along south side of Danube River against heavy opposition. Combat Command R advanced southwest along north side of Danube River, contacted elements 63rd Infantry

Division and 4th Infantry Division. Relieved from mission and moved to reinforce the bridgehead south of the Danube River. Estimated 2456 prisoners taken.

April 26—Combat Command A moved southeast to relieve cavalry elements securing a bridge in the vicinity of Hiltenfingen. Combat Command B moved to help elements of the 63rd Infantry Division repel counter-attack in their bridgehead. 101st Cavalry Group attacked southeast from the vicinity of Burgau and advanced rapidly. Troop B. 92nd Cavalry Reconnaissance Squadron captured a bridge intact across the Wertach River in the vicinity of Hiltenfingen. Captured 828 prisoners (including one major general), two 88-mm guns, twelve nebelwerfers, forty to fifty ME 262's (approximately twenty in working condition), one plane assembly plant, one ammunition dump and other materiel and motor transport.

April 27—Combat Command R cleared towns of Kirch Sienbnach, Siebnach, Ettringen, Markt Wald, Immelstetten and Neufnach. 2800 Allied prisoners of war freed, including 1400 Americans. Division continued advance to the east, crossing Wertach River, prepared to cross Lech River. 5200 prisoners, two hospitals with 1300 patients, four nebelwerfers, 125 vehicles, twelve anti-aircraft guns, an airfield with 60-80 planes, quartermaster and signal warehouses captured.

April 28—101st Cav Group crossed repaired railroad bridge over Lech River and took Landsberg. 10,051 prisoners of war and a military hospital with 1400 patients captured. Division Command Post opened at Schwabmuenchen.

April 29—Combat Command A made junction with elements 10th Armored Division at Oberau at 2000B. Went to assembly area south of Murnau. Combat Command B crossed Lech River and reached Weilheim. Division Command Post opened at Landsberg airfield at 1630B. 3261 prisoners taken.

April 30—Combat Command B continued advance to southeast until reaching Durnhausen and Schlendorf. Halted by seven bridges blown in their path. Combat Command R cleared area between Ammer and Wurm Sees. 865 prisoners captured. Combat Command V of the French 2nd Armored Division attached to the 12th Armored Division.

May 1— Combat Command R advanced down Autobahn to Inn River. 1400 prisoners taken.

May 2—Combat Command R continued reconnaissance to south along Inn River. Combat Command V (French) crossed bridge at Bad Tolz. Remainder of Division in assembly areas awaiting orders. Estimated 8000 prisoners taken.

May 3—Combat Command R continued advance along Inn River valley, encountering strong passive resistance. 23rd Tank Battalion crossed Inn River and continued attack to the south, crossing Austrian border at 1318. Combat Command V (French) attacked against light resistance toward Berchtesgaden. Advance Division Command Post opened vicinity Redenfelden. 12,060 prisoners processed through Division cage.

May 4—Combat Command R relieved in position by elements of the 36th Infantry Division. Combat Command V (French) continued advance east along autobahn meeting strong passive resistance. 8,216 prisoners taken.

May 5—Last Day of Combat. Division Command Post opened at Heidenheim.

May 6—Division closed in occupation area. Commenced maintenance and rehabilitation and occupation duties.

APPENDIX B

Those Left Behind

Although the 12th Armored Division was in combat for only five months, its members paid a steep price for their service to our country. During their time overseas, one Hellcat in three became a casualty. Some men were injured in accidents, or wounded or captured in battle. Others became incapacitated by trench foot or pneumonia, or other illnesses.

The men listed below died in the service of our country. Dates of death are listed if known. The final resting place if known, is also listed. All who served gave of themselves; these gave all they had.

Last Name	First Name	Co	Died	Buried
17th Armored Infantry Battalion				
Algiere	Biaso A	B		
Allen	Harry		May 2,1945	
Anderson	Merle O.	B		
Apsey	Charles	C		
Archer	Opal M.	C		
Bacola	Simon S.	A		
Bafare	Leonard W.	Hq		
Bane	Charles C.	C		
Barker	George W.	C	Jan 16,1945	
Bassininsky	Peter	B		
Bellanger	Erwin	C		
Benny	James I	C		
Berkel	Kenneth J	B		
Bird	Enos	C		
Bisgeier	Bernard	C		
Blackford	Harold J.	A		
Booth	Harold G.	C		
Brandvold	Anton O.	A	Jan 17,1945	
Breaud	Odelle L.	A	Apr 5,1945	
Breidigan	Leo	C		
Brenner	Marks J.	C	Dec 9,1944	
Brewster	Robert E.			
Brown	Willie W.		Jan 18,1945	
Bruno	Alfred	C		
Bryant	Elvis W.	C	Jan 16,1945	
Buccino	James V.	C		

Last Name	First Name	Co	Died	Buried
Bucher, Jr	AlexanderJ.	C	Feb 4,1945	
Burt	Thomas H.	A	Apr 1,1945	
Cale	Hamilton N	A		
Cameron	Albert	C		
Cameron	David R.	C		
Cape	James H.	B	Apr 10,1945	
Caplinger	James M.	A	Mar 23,1945	
Carrell	Gordon T.	C		
Carroll	Richard R.	C		
Christopherson	James W.	B		
Cichon	John T.	B		
Ciocchi	Frank A.	B		
Clemans	Elmer	B		
Coakley	John S.	B		
Cochran	Harold	B		
Coen	Alonzo L	B		
Cole	Verland	C		
Collier	Charles R.	C	Apr 26,1945	
Connolley	Patrick	C		
Cook	John C.	C		
Crandall	Robert J.	C		
Crawford	James E.	A		
Cronin	Johnathan	B		
Curry	Willard M.	B		
Dalessandro	Michael			
Dambrosio	Hector A.		Dec 10,1944	
Davis	Cecil A.	B	Mar 23,1945	
Deck	Harry W.	C		
Decker	Eugene H.	C		
DeYoung	Marinus	C		
Dickinson	Charles M.	C		
DiDia	Carl	C		
Dillingham	Elzy L.	C		
Dirks	HeneryV.	A	Jan 19,1945	
Dombroski	Joe W.	A	Jan 18,1945	
Dowl	Alexander B.			
Dusina	Amos	A	Jan 19,1945	
Eckert	Andrew H.	A	May 3,1945	
Eckoff	Lester	B		
Edgren	Robert E.		Feb 5,1945	
Edwards	Jesse H.	B	Jan 18,1945	

Last Name	First Name	Co	Died	Buried
Englander	Bruce	A		
Ervin	Robert J.		Oct 29,1944	
Fordyce	Owen J.	A		
Fortunati	Dario	A		
Freeman	Loyd	B		
Frymire	Durrell S.	B		
Fuchs	John E.	A		
Garay	John	B		
Gardner	Clarence E.	A		
Gau	Harold R.	B		
Gerbe	Edward	B		
Gill	Alberto	A	Apr 5,1945	
Gile	Edman B.	B		
Gough	Austin C.			
Greer	Malcolm T.	B		
Griffith	Thomas J.	A		
Guckert	Robert	B		
Gulesano	Salvatore	C		
Gunyon	Hollis J.	C		
Habeman	Edwin I	B		
Hagan	John E.	C		
Hager	Clyde A.		Apr 5,1945	
Haller	Eugene	B		
Hamann	Elwin	C		
Hammond	James R.	C		
Harkins	Joe	B		
Harrington	Luther B	B		
Hash	Raymond	B		
Haufle	John	B		
Heelas	Jack	B		
Heltenberg	Walter R.	A		
Henderson	Leo G.	B	Jan 16,1945	
Homer, Jr	Philip L.	C		
Hosek	John	C	Apr 12,1945	
Jacob	Oliver	B		
Jacobs	Harold	B		
Jarrell	Bretram	C		
Jeske	Harold	B	Jan 18,1945	
Johnson	Benjamin	B		
Johnson	Dennis E.	C	Dec 9,1944	
Johnson	John L	C		

Last Name	First Name	Co	Died	Buried
Kapelke	Benjamin	C		
Katz	Alton H.	C	Jan 16,1945	
Kent	Willis E.	A		
Kessler	Ernest V.	A	Jan 18,1945	
Ketchledge	Bert	A		
Kling	Paul A		Jan 19,1945	
Lakin	Richard L.	Hq		
Lareau	Mahlon	C		
Larthey	Francis A.	C		
Lembke	John	B		
Litwak	Morris	B		
Lonergan	Thomas J H	B		
Lynbarger	Ralph E.	A		
Mariluch	Adrian W.	A	Jan 19,1945	
Maxey	Luther L.	C		
Maximov	Martin J.		Apr 5,1945	
McCandlish	Robert	C		
McClorey	John J	C		
McGann	Edward L.	A		
Mears	William	C		
Miller	Paul J.	B		
Miller	Wilbur O.	B	Dec 10,1944	
Mitchell,Jr	Edward J.	A		
Muir	Milton W.	C		
Mullikin	Clarence E.	A	Jan 18,1945	
Mervi	David			
Miller	Harles	B		
Nedwied	William J	C		
Notzke	Kenneth W			
O'Callaghan	Donnell P	B		
O'Neil	Robert G	B	Jan 16,1945	
O'Neil	Thomas C	B		
Oaks	Francis E.	C		
Okin	Leslie	B		
Olson	Marshall A.	B		
Ostrach	Edward A.	A	Jan 17,1945	
Patterson	Daniel T.	B	Apr 2,1945	
Peiper	Charles J.	C		
Perrigo	Bruce F.	B		
Phillinger	John	B		
Phillips	Alonzo W.			

Last Name	First Name	Co	Died	Buried
Piwok	Stephen J.	C	Dec. 8, 1945	
Place	Millard J.	C		
Poff	Gillus V	B		
Polo	William	B		
Prieto	Jerry	B		
Pronge	Willie F.	B		
Ragland	Junius J B	A		
Ramirez	Pete A.	B	Mar 19,1945	
Ramirez	Santos	A	Mar 23,1945	
Ramsey	William A.	A		
Reierson	Wilson A.	A		
Richardson	George P.	B		
Ridenour	Richard L.	B	Dec 9,1944	
Riker	Andrew W	B	Dec 10,1944	
Robinson	John H.		Apr 10,1945	
Rogers	Joseph L.	B		
Roney	Karol E	B	Apr 2,1945	
Sanchez	Lester D.	C		
Schell	Hollis D.	B		
Smith	Laurence	B		
Schirato	Aldo T.	B	Feb 6,1945	
Schnese	Flavian J.	B	Apr 1,1945	
Schumaker	George L.	A		
Shawver	Thomas E	B		
Slage	Clarence R.	Hq		
Smith	Fred L.	C	Apr 6,1945	
Smith	Norman D.	C		
Smith	William B.	C		
Sohodski	Edward	A	Apr 12,1945	
Sorbo	Michael	C		
Spatola,Jr	Sante S			
Stanier	Joseph R.	C	Dec 9,1944	
Starr	Robert M.	B	Feb 5,1945	
Starziski	John	C	Jan 16,1945	
Stone	Eugene M.			
Stygar	John A.	C		
Swackhamer	William A.	A	Jan 19,1945	
Tee	Robert M.	C		
Thompson	Ashley C N	A		
Thornhill	Clarence D	Hq	Apr 24,1945	
Torgerson	Gerald O	C		

Last Name	First Name	Co	Died	Buried
Tramontano	Frank	C		
Trittipo	Thomas A.	B		
Verotsko	George R.	C		
Wadsworth	Glenn G	A		
Walter	William F.	C		
Warren	Raymond	B		
Wasylkiw	Leo M.	C		
Waugerman	Roy G	B		
Weaver	Albert L.			
Williams	Garland			
Williamson	Bob C	A	Apr 12,1945	
Wilmeth	Tom T.	B	Apr 22,1945	
Wilson	Robert W.	A		Lorraine
Wilson	Tracy	A		
Wojciechowski	Julius R.	C	Jan 16,1945	Epinal
Wojcik	Edward P	B		
Wolfe	Egbert B.			
Wolfhope	Mark	A		
Wood	Charles C.	C	Apr 12,1945	Lorraine
Wortkowski	Sigmund P.	Hq	Apr 1,1945	Lorraine
Zavatsky	John F.	B	Feb 4,1945	Epinal
Zisa	John b.	B		
Zurawski	Edward L.	B		

23rd Tank Battalion

Last Name	First Name	Co	Died	Buried
Adams	Carl J.	Hq	Dec 10,1944	
Amiot	Robert			Lorraine
Amos	Gilbert E.	D		Lorraine
Ayers	Richard W.	C	Mar 23,1945	Lorraine
Beach	Harry M.			
Bow	John L.			
Braaten	Bjarne		Jan 18,1945	Epinal
Brown	William E.			
Bumgarner	Sam J.		Mar 31,1945	Lorraine
Chruma	Frank S.			
Cook	Robert L.	C	Apr 10,1945	Lorraine
Cowan	Donald B.	B	Dec 9,1945	Lorraine
Croft	Edgar L.			
Dellinger	Cleavorn H.			
Detrick	Kenneth J.	C		
Dickey	Merle G.	C		

Last Name	First Name	Co	Died	Buried
Dolence	Albin J.		Jan 17,1945	Epinal
Doughty	Marion L.		Mar 19,1945	Lorraine
Dudley	Orville R.			
Entwisle	Robert E.		Jan 18,1945	Epinal
Forrester	Judson R.		Dec 17,1945	Lorraine
Gialuisi	Joseph			
Green	Gothie H.		Mar 19,1945	Lorraine
Greims	Arthur W.,Jr.		Dec 10,1944	Lorraine
Griffith	Floyd A.		Jan 17,1945	Epinal
Guitteau	Wayne F.	C		
Henn	John L.		Mar 19,1945	Lorraine
Hicks	Virgil E			
Hilemon	Ward F.			
Humpherys	Donald L.	D		
Jackson	James R.		Jan 18,1945	Epinal
Kempf	Philiip W.	A	Apr 22,1945	Lorraine
Knapp	Lawrence J.			
Koob	William E.		Dec 10,1945	Lorraine
Kramer	Marion M.		Jan 14,1945	Epinal
Lange	Albert C.,Jr.	A	Jan 18,1945	Epinal
Lingscheit	Ronald W.		Mar 19,1945	Lorraine
Linneman	Francis J.		Mar 19,1945	Lorraine
Little	Walter J.		Apr 12,1945	Lorraine
Manson	William T.		Mar 19,1945	Lorraine
Mattinen	Harvey R.			
McCurdy	Robert E.		Feb 4,1945	Epinal
McFerren	Maynard	C	Apr 1,1945	Lorraine
Megis	Montgomery C.	Hq	Dec 11,1945	Lorraine
Milak	Emerson J.		Mar 31,1945	Lorraine
Murphy	Thomas P.			
O'Brian	Timmothy F.	C	Apr 4,1945	Lorraine
Ogburn	E.F.		Mar 19,1945	Epinal
Paglia	Eugene			
Pazone	Vincent A.			
Patterson	Warren H.	A		
Perrino	Frank		Mar 19,1945	Lorraine
Poole	John J.			
Powell	John E.		Mar 31,1945	Lorraine
Raines	Billy T.	C	Apr 1,1945	Lorraine
Rebhun	Jerome J.			
Reents	Lyle G.			

Last Name	First Name	Co	Died	Buried
Reitano	Edward S.,Jr.	C		
Rhoades	Cletus C.	D	Mar 31,1945	Epinal
Rosenqvist	Mark D.	Hq	Dec 10,1944	Lorraine
Russell	George W.			
Ryan	Patrick J.			
Seabaugh	Bland F.,Jr.			
Sisler	Junior D.			
Springer	Jesse		Apr 10,1945	Lorraine
Storey	Maurice J.	C		
Tenney	George J.	C	Dec 10,1944	Lorraine
Thomas	James F.,Jr.			
Varney	Elmo	A		
Vickless	Edward P.	C		
Welch	James A.	C	Apr 10,1945	Lorraine
Wolke	Alvin		Mar 31,1945	Lorraine

43rd Tank Battalion

Last Name	First Name	Co	Died	Buried
Berry	Roy	B	Apr 9,1945	Lorraine
Braen	Hermann C.	C		
Buckingham	Louis W.	A		
Busby	Grover C.	A		
Buzard	Hilton F.	D		
Cahalan	Jeremiah R.	D		
Cantillion	Joseph M.	C	Jan 17,1945	Lorraine
Clapp	Crover F.	B		
Coleman	Thomas H.,Jr.	A	Jan 16,1945	Epinal
Colton	George D.	A	Jan 16,1945	Epinal
Corcoran	Earle E.	Hq	Jan 16,1945	Epinal
Creamer	John F.	C		
Cullen	Eugene C.	A		
DilMenna	Frank	A		
Drury	Francis P.	B	Mar 21,1945	Lorraine
Duggan	Jess W.	B		
Gilbert	Melvyn B.	Hq		
Gilleland	Charles M.	C		
Gossey	Roscoe L.	C	Mar 24,1945	Lorraine
Goyak	Thomas S.	Hq		
Grant	Gerald	A		
Green	Kenneth L.	Hq		
Gregory	Robert S	C		
Hackworth	Robert F	D	Apr 10,1945	Lorraine

Last Name	First Name	Co	Died	Buried
Haigler	Richard W.	D		
Halm	Russell I	C	Jan 17,1945	Ardennes
Harper	Albert F	B		
Hartman	Norman R.	C		
Hatcher	Cecil R.	B		
Healy	Lester E.	C		
Herzberg	James	Hq	Apr 6,1945	Lorraine
Hokkanen	George M.	C	Jan 17,1945	Epinal
Honebrink	Anton J.	A		
Hood	Harry W.	D		
Johnson	Jack B	B	Jan 17,1945	Epinal
Jones	Carlton E.	D		
Keeves	Max	B		
Kieffer	William J.	A	Jan 17,1945	Epinal
Kilcheski	John J.	B		
Kostraba	Alfred A.	B	Apr 24,1945	Lorraine
Kraemer	Paul A. M.	Hq	Jan 16,1945	Epinal
Kulp	Russell E	B		
Lemley	Abe L	D		
Lopez	Jesse E.	B	Jan 17,1945	Epinal
Malecke	William B	D	Jan 21,1945	Epinal
Mann	Jack D	A		
Marfio	Peter T.	C		
McConnell	Willie E.	C	Jan 16,1945	Epinal
McShane	James J.	A	Jan 17,1945	Epinal
Merkle	Gerald A.	Sv		
Mihalko	James	C	Jan 17,1945	Epinal
Miller	George C.	D		
Monastra	Salvatore S.	B	Feb 4,1945	Lorraine
Moss	Roy W.	A	Dec 10,1945	Lorraine
Pendleton	Paul S.	B		
Pluchta	Joseph	B	Mar 21,1945	Lorraine
Polson	Rueben W.	C	Jan 16,1945	Epinal
Robbins	Harold L.	A		
Roberts	Dale S.	C		
Robertson	Francis E.	C		
Root	Rodney R.	C	Feb 4,1945	Epinal
Schwartz	Joseph	B		
Shepard	Howard A.	A		
Snyder	Earl M.	C		Epinal
Spanier	William A.	A	Mar 23,1945	Ardennes

Last Name	First Name	Co	Died	Buried
Stillman	Ray W.	Hq	Apr 9,1945	Lorraine
Stout	Robert N.	D		
Stshwokes	Stanley D.	Hq	Apr 10,1945	Lorraine
Tardie	Clifford	B	Mar 30,1945	Lorraine
Tarwater	Lacy D.	D		
Wasson	John T.	C	Jan 17,1945	Epinal
Williams	Robet O.	A		Epinal
White	William T.			

44th Tank Battalion

Last Name	First Name			Buried
Bumka	Frank L.			
Boucher	Kenneth L.			Manila
Brewer	Clifton S.			
Brophy	Arnold E.			
Busta	Edward F.			Manila
Campbell	Donald			
Candler	Arthur A.			Manila
Carrington	Roy K.			
Carver	Otha L.			
Chesser	James W.			
Cinotti	William			
Donath	Donald			
Fisher	Raymond			Manila
Gallant	John G.			
Griffin	Daniel			Manila
Howard	Burton E.			Manila
Hummel	Raymond H.			Manila
Inverson	Maurice			
King	John L. Jr.			Manila
Lipps	Clair J			Manila
Losinski	Florian			
Lyle	Hershal A.			
Myers	Wilbert J.			
Minton	John R.			
Muklewicz	James J.			Manila
Nagy	William P.			
Reinartz	Leo F.			
Rogic	John C.			
Ross	Tom H.			
Rusin	George			
Spaul	Wilbur L.			
Willis	Lee V.			

56th Armored Infantry Battalion

Last Name	First Name	Co	Died	Buried
Abney	Clarence L.	B	Jan 18,1945	Epinal
Aellig	Wilmer E.			
Allison,Jr	Edgar W.		Jan 17,1945	Lorraine
Amason	William C.	A	Apr 4,1945	Lorraine
Ancell	Wilford L.		Apr 1,1945	Lorraine
Anderson	John F.		Feb 7,1945	Epinal
Anderson	Walter O.	B		
Astour	Edward	B		
Baquet	Paul C.	B		
Barnes	Gerald W.	A	Jan 16,1945	Epinal
Barnes, Jr	James G.			
Barnett	Jack L.	A		
Barry	Edward E.	A		
Bassett	Jay		Jan 9,1945	Epinal
Bastty	Edward E.			Lorraine
Blackburn	John T.		Apr 25,1945	
Blair	Clyde J.	A		
Blake, Jr	James E.			
Blodgett	James P.		Apr 8,1945	Epinal
Boch	Richard A		Mar 31,1945	Lorraine
Bourne	Eugene S.			
Bowman	Philip R.			
Brisco	Douglas J.		Mar 21,1945	
Brown	Melvin			
Bubb	Merlyn R.			
Carrigan	Billy E.	C	Jan 8,1945	
Castronova	Nicholas J.		Feb 5,1945	Epinal
Chavez	Felix M.	B		
Churry	Albert	A		
Clifford	Edward M.	B		
Clingermna	Hugh A.	A	Jan 16,1945	Lorraine
Clough	John H.			
Cook	Odell B.			
Cooper	Howard R.	B		
Darnell	Delbert C.	B		
Dawes	George C.	A		
DeMeo	Anthony J.	B	Jan 18,1945	Epinal
Desmond	William P.		Jan 17,1945	Lorraine
Dicks	Carl J.			

Last Name	First Name	Co	Died	Buried
Dillon	Neville L.	A	Dec 21,1944	Lorraine
Dukich	Nicholas	A	Jan 10,1945	
Dumas	Russell D			
Eddy	Harold R.			
Egan	Richard C.			
Emery	Everett L.	A		
Erber,Jr.	Emil G.	A	Jan 9,1945	
Fintel	Hubet A.		Apr 15,1945	Lorraine
Fonger	Maynard P.	Hq	Jan 9,1945	
France	William A.			
Frueh,Jr	Albert W.			
Furman	Richard K.	B	Jan 15,1945	Epinal
Gabree	John W.			
Gagliardi	Salver G.	B		Lorraine
Gaherty	Thomas A.	A	Dec 21,1944	
Garcia	Jore M.			
Gill	Walter H.	B		
Glover	James H.	D		
Grobe	Rober L.		Apr 18,1945	Lorraine
Groves	William B.			
Gutierrez	Roberto H.	B	Jan 18,1945	Epinal
Haden	Carl E.	B		
Halcomb	Hugh A.	B		
Hazmuka	Leo C.	B		
Heaberlin	Harry P.	B		
Henderson	James W.			
Hickey	Robert A.	B	Jan 31,1945	Lorraine
Hilgert	Henry	B		
Hill	Robert I.	A		
Hoff	Wilford D.			
Hollingsworth	James C.			
Holmes	Ernest H.		Apr 25,1945	
Hornbeck	Donald C.	B		
Horne	Robert E.			
Hulsizer	Frank B.	B		
Inpson	LaurenceT.			
Irak	Joseph A.		Apr 4,1945	Lorraine
Jacobson	Al			
Jakstis	Stephen J.			
Johnson	Carl O.	A	Jan 16,1945	Epinal
Jones	Carl O.	C		

Last Name	First Name	Co	Died	Buried
Kasnachey	Edward	B	Jan 18,1945	Epinal
Kempter, Jr	Jacob			
Kirkham	Benjamin G.		Jan 16,1945	Epinal
Kline	Gordan A.			
Koceniak	John J.			
Krueger	Bert T.	C	Jan 8,1945	
Kubiak	Stanley S.	C	Jan 14,1945	Epinal
Lane	Clinton M.	B	Jan 16,1945	Epinal
LeRoux	Francis C.		Apr 15,1945	Lorraine
Lesniak	Frank S.			
Lopez	John P.			
LoPresti	Aurther J.			
Lymberis	John	B		
Lytle	Herman J.	D		
MacKinlay	Bruce S.			
Maestes	John N.		Jan 11,1945	
Malinkowski,Jr	F.M.			
Martin	Warren I.	A	Dec 21,1944	Lorraine
Mattox	James M.	B		
Michael	William E.	B	Jan 18,1945	Lorraine
Miller	Thomas E.			
Mithell	George J.			
Moore	Walter W.			
Motteram	Maurice	A	Jan 9,1945	
Murphy	Eugene D.			
Myers	James D.		Jan 17,1945	Lorraine
Myers	Lewis G.		Apr 18,1945	Lorraine
Neal	Bernard G.	B		
Neiman	George P.			
Novak	Stephen	B	Jan 11,1945	Epinal
Nowinski	Daniel A.			
Oliver	Seth T.	B		
Palma	Alex A			
Patterson,Jr.	John	A		
Pelland	George E.			
Perrotte	William E.	B	Jan 18,1945	Epinal
Poff	Charles W.			
Quick	LeGrande E.	C	Jan 8,1945	
Recoy	Kenneth W.			
Reider	Ralph L.		Jan 9,1945	Epinal
Reynolds	James D.	C	Jan 8,1945	

Last Name	First Name	Co	Died	Buried
Rick	Fred B.	B		
Robinson	James P.			
Roleson	Carroll W.			
Rotger	Ralph A.	A		
Roth	Marvin			
Roth	Warren G.	B		
Rumberger	Walter E.			
Russell	Richard L.			
Schacatano	Joseph	A	Jan 16,1945	Lorraine
Schaefer	Albert W.		Jan 14,1945	Epinal
Schmidt	Carl S.			
Schroyer	Lawrence E.			
Sharr	Donald J.			
Sheesley	Charles D.			
Sifuentes	Nicasio C.			
Sillery	James A.	A	Jan 9,1945	Epinal
Silverling	Leslie T.	C		
Speers	John A. D.		Jan 17,1945	Epinal
springer	Keith F.	C	Jan 14,1945	
Steiger	Elden E.			
Stone	Leonard H.	B	Jan 22,1945	Lorraine
Swartz	FranklinW.		Jan 17,1945	Lorraine
Sykvester	Miller	A	May 3,1945	Epinal
Taylor	Leo E.			
Taylor	LeRoy J.		Jan 9,1945	Epinal
Theilen	Harold R.		Jan 17,1945	Lorraine
Tornquist	Gordan E..	Hq	Jan 9,1945	
Tuzzolino	Frank M.		Apr 5,1945	Lorraine
Wells	Harold K.			
Whitting	Oscar E.			
Williams	Henry N.			
Willis	Charles M.	A	Mar 24,1945	Lorraine
Winkler	Robert J.			
Wollemburg	Orville L.			
Zandona	Robert B.	B	Jan 10,1945	Epinal

66th Armored Infantry Battalion

Abrahamson	Roy E.	A		
Adamaitis	Joseph J.		Apr 29,1945	Lorraine
Archer	William		Mar 31,1945	Lorraine
Ashley	Carlos E.	C	Jan 16,1945	Epinal
Atkins	William S.	A		

Last Name	First Name	Co	Died	Buried
Atkinson	Willard W.	C	Apr 11,1945	Lorraine
Avery	Erwin	C		
Bale	William J.	C		
Barents	Albertus	C	Jan 16,1945	Epinal
Bark	Allen J.	B	Mar 22,1945	Lorraine
Barron	John			
Beisman	Carl	C	Jan 20,1945	Lorraine
Berka, Jr	Mark J.	C	Jan 16,1945	Epinal
Berman	Milton	C		
Bird	Virgil T.	B		
Blankenship	John W.	A	Jan 16,1945	Epinal
Bloom	Sydney	C?		
Boehler	Theaphil	A	Apr 7,1945	Lorraine
Boehm	Gregory F.	C	Jan 16,1945	Epinal
Booth	William J.	C	Jan 16,1945	Epinal
Borger	Lester S.	C		
Brown	Franklin R.	C		
Brown	Jack C.	C		
Brown, Jr.	Oliver A.	C	Jan 16,1945	Epinal
Buchan	Scott W.	C		
Burson	Douglas L.	B		
Byron	Buford D.	B		
Cahill	Richard G.	A	Jan 16,1945	Epinal
Caldwell	Donald H.	B	Mar 30,1945	
Carlson	LeRoy E.			
Chayt	Albert I.		Jan 19,1945	Epinal
Chaytor	Clarence G.	C	Jan 16,1945	Epinal
Chilcutt	Charles C.	C		
Christenson	Arthur W.	C		
Clark	James H.	C	Jan 16,1945	Epinal
Collinsworth	Delbert	C		
Corley	John H.		Apr 1,1945	Lorraine
Deal	Verlie P.	C		
Diehl	Arthur A.		Apr 8,1945	Lorraine
Dixon	Robert L.	B		
Dreusike	Robert F	A	Jan 22,1945	Epinal
Dunaway	Alfred	C		
Duncan	Francis C.	C		
Dunn	Francis L.	B		
Elrick	Richard G.	C	Jan 16,1945	Epinal

Last Name	First Name	Co	Died	Buried
Erck,Jr.	Charles F.	A		
Evans	Hermand D.	C		
Framke	Paul O.H.		Apr 6,1945	Lorraine
Frazier	Wilson I.	A	Jan 16,1945	Epinal
Friedman	Merkel	B		
Gahagan	Bernard P.	C		
Gervais	Louise C.	C	Jan 16,1945	
Gonska	Edwar J.	C		
Gonzales	Phillip	C		
Goodwin	Harold R.	C	Apr 10,1945	Lorraine
Gough	Max	C	Jan 25,1945	Epinal
Grandy	Doyle R.			
Grubba	Raymond J.	C		
Gufstsfson	Roland H.	B		
Gumm	Howard F.	Hq	Jan 19,1945	Epinal
Gunnoe	Edsel W.		Apr 11,1945	Lorraine
Guthrie	Edward H.	C		
Hall	Raymond F.			
Hansen	Alvin D.	C	Jan 16,1945	Epinal
Heneghen	Lawrence M.		Apr 26,1945	Lorraine
Heyer	Walter	A	Jan 16,1945	Epinal
Higgins	Robert E.	C	Jan 16,1945	Epinal
Hojan	Frank L.	A	Mar 21,1945	Lorraine
Holmes	Ernest H.			Lorraine
Horne	William E.		Mar 24,1945	Lorraine
Houghton	William	C	Jan 16,1945	Epinal
Houston	Thomas L.	C	Jan 16,1945	Epinal
Huff	Glenn E.	B	Mar 23,1945	Lorraine
Hunter	John R.	C		
Irwin	Willard E.		Apr 28,1945	Lorraine
Jardine	Robert	A		
Johnson	Dennis			
Johnson	James E.	C		
Johnson	Jimmie C.	C?		
Johnson	Maynard E.	B		
Jones	James D.	C		
Joseph	Burson W.	C	Jan 16,1945	Epinal
Jura	John M.	B	Apr 21,1945	Lorraine
Kain	Robert J.	C		
Kelley	Albert L.	B		
King	Millard S.	C		

Last Name	First Name	Co	Died	Buried
Kingery	Elbert D.		Apr 11,1945	Lorraine
Kinnard, Jr.	Jerry B.		Apr 17,1945	Lorraine
Kircher,Jr	Harry L.			
Krupowitz	Benjamin W.	C	Jan 16,1945	Epinal
Kwaitkoski	Clarence			
LaPatka	James F.	B		
Lassiter	Haskell R.		Dec 8,1944	Lorraine
Littler	John R.	B	Mar 30,1945	Lorraine
Loftis	Victor M.		Apr 3,1945	Lorraine
Looser	Ceral J.	B	Jan 19,1945	Epinal
Lucas	Emory O.	C	Apr 24,1945	Lorraine
Lydon, Jr	Thomas N.	B	Apr 9,1945	Lorraine
Macintire	William I.			
Maestas	John N.		Jan 11,1945	Epinal
Mancill	Allen M.	C		
McCauley	Edward J.	C		
McDonough	Martin T.	C		
Miner	Robert B.	A		
Mondelblatt	Elmwood W.	C	Jan 16,1945	Epinal
Moore	Ernest W.	A		
Nelson	Nathaniel O.		Apr 2,1945	Lorraine
Nelson	Travis C		Dec 21,1944	Lorraine
Oelz	George R		Jan 19,1945	Epinal
Orzel	Mathew J	C		
Oxendine	Asberry G	C		
Patriquin,Jr.	Royal B	A	Jan 20,1945	Lorraine
Patterson, Jr.	John	A		
Popek	Carl	SV		
Powell	Claude J			
Prest	Roy W	C		
Rankey, Jr	James R	A		
Reed	Russell K	C	Jan 16,1945	Lorraine
Reggins	Paul A	A		
Rielly	James J	A	Jan 16,1945	Epinal
Riddick	Thomas L.		Apr 24,1945	Lorraine
Ringuette	Leo J	B		
Roszman	John P	C		
Rundle	Thomas W	C	Jan 16,1945	Epinal
Russell	Leon A	B		
Ryan	William E.	C		
Schalla	Leslie G	A		

Last Name	First Name	Co	Died	Buried
Schlund	Gordon E	C		
Schultz, Jr.	Charles R	C		
Schwerdtfeger	Herbert		Apr 28,1945	Lorraine
Scott	Horace N	A		
Shulman	Irving L			
Simons	Glen A	C		Lorraine
Slomka	Irving	C		
Steffensen	Wesely R	C		
Stringham	Walter P	A	Dec 8,1944	Lorraine
Strychasz	Stanley J	C	Apr 1,1945	Lorraine
Sulli	Peter A	B	Jan 19,1945	Epinal
Sullivan	James V	B		
Szymoniak	Frank T	B	Apr 21,1945	Lorraine
Thatcher	George C	C	Jan 16,1945	Epinal
Tomasello	Albert T	C		
Vitanovitz	Stephen F	C		
Vogel	Lewis A			
Walker	William H	C	Apr 11,1945	Lorraine
Warren	Jasper F	A	Mar 21,1945	Lorraine
Washington	Dink		Apr 24,1945	Lorraine
Watley	John		Apr 23,1945	Lorraine
Watson	Lloyd G	C	Jan 16,1945	Epinal
Weaver	Charles G.	C		
Westphal	Robert W	C	Jan 16,1945	Epinal
Wojcik	Frank	C		
Wooley	Woodrow W.	A	Apr 7,1945	Epinal
Wortinger	Keith A.			
Zaroni	Thomas F.	A		

82nd Armored Medical Battalion

Dalton	Robert A.	B	Apr 23,1945	Lorraine
Edge	John E.	A		
Golden	Edward J.	B		
Pittari	Joseph L.	B		

92nd Cavalry Reconnaissance Squadron

Adelman	Samuel	A		
Anderson	Reuben C.	D		
Aters, Jr.	Walter E.	B		
Baldwin	Edwin E.	D		
Black	Frederico A.	A	Apr 27,1945	Lorraine

Last Name	First Name	Co	Died	Buried
Buhrle	Charles K.	C		
Calderon	Dennis R.	B		
Capra	William	F		
Chapron	Armand L.	B	Apr 22,1945	Lorraine
Clary	Cecil T.	B	Mar 8,1945	Epinal
Cohen	Bernard	E	Apr 26,1945	Lorraine
Dobson	Donald H.	D		
Farrell	Bruce J.	C		
Kerstetter	John W.	Med	Mar 31,1945	Lorraine
Lannon	Edward J.	C	Dec 22,1944	Lorraine
Larson	William J.	C		
Lubas	Chester J.	A		
Maddock	Edward B.	D	Apr 5,1945	Lorraine
Madl	Joseph J.	E		
Madhouse	Willard W.	B	Apr 5,1945	Lorraine
McGuff	David E.	C		
McLaughlin	Cloyce F.	C	Apr 14,1945	Lorraine
Michaels	Theodore J.	A	Apr 24,1945	Lorraine
Mozzetti	Patrick	F		
Nolen	John N.	C		
Olszewski	Frank V.	B	Jan 14,1945	Epinal
Paladin	Edward J.	B		
Pasquali	James	A		
Perrone	Alfred J.	B	Apr 12,1945	Lorraine
Peterman	Joseph J.	A	Apr 20,1945	Lorraine
Pietropaold	Alex D.	A		
Puskas	Zoltan	F		
Radney	Irwin C.	B	Jan 13,1945	Epinal
Rickard	Harold L.	A		
Rickell	Harold W.	A		
Ripp	Edwin J.	C		
Romanski	Rudolph	C		
Schulman	Sidney	D		
Simonson	John F.	E	Apr 5,1945	Lorraine
Spors	Russell P.	A	Mar 29,1945	Lorraine
Stevenson	Cecil R.	C		
TenHagen	Russell B.	A	Mar 17,1945	Luxembourg
Thatcher	Benjamin E.	C	Jan 17,1945	Epinal
Thornton	Dale H.	C	Apr 12,1945	Lorraine
Yee	Tung L.	B		

Last Name	First Name	Co	Died	Buried

119th Engineer Battalion

Last Name	First Name	Co	Died	Buried
Arndt	Immanuel W., PFC		Jan. 19, 1945	
Baker	Victor A., CPL	C	Jan 19,1945	Epinal
Baysinger	Archie S J.			
Bentley	Robert H. 2LT		Jan 17,1945	Epinal
Bosich	Peter A., T5		Jan 16,1945	Epinal
Brandon	George G., T5		April 13,1945	Ardennes
Buchanon	Linzie J.			
Carmody	Joseph P.	C		
Cicchetti	Louis A., SSGT	C	Jan 17,1945	Epinal
Duncan	Ninian, 1LT	C	Jan 19,1945	Lorraine
Finkbeiner	Donald J.	C		
Heydt	Lloyd I., Sgt		Jan 17,1945	Epinal-MIA
Johnson	Edward L.. PFC	B	Apr 19,1945	Lorraine
Kemp	Thomas H.			
Kill	Albert			
Kuhni	Joseph L., Pfc		Jan 19,1945	Lorraine
Martin,Jr	Thomas H., Capt	C	Feb 8,1945	Lorraine
McConnell	James H.		Apr 4,1945	
Ouimette	Francis W.			
Rightmire	Roy, T5		Mar 10,1945	Epinal
Schoening	Thomas F., PFC		Jan 19,1945	Epinal
Stevens	Stacy E.			
Strek	Bernard S.	C		
Trujillo	Leo J., Pvt	C	Jan 19,1945	Epinal
Wudel	Herman W, T5		Feb 4,1945	Epinal

134th Ordnance Battalion

Last Name	First Name	Co	Died	Buried
Collins	Stanley		Apr 19,1945	
McMahan	Marvin E.			
Schmitt	Paul J.			
Secord	Asa E.		Jun 30,1945	
Winje	Vernal	C	Aug 1,1945	

152nd Signal Company

Last Name	First Name	Co	Died	Buried
Milam	Corneal F		Jun 13,1945	

493rd Armored Field Artillery Battalion

Last Name	First Name	Btry	Died	Buried
Carter	Everett C.	Hq		

Last Name	First Name	Co	Died	Buried
Elliott	Emmett T.	B	Apr 10,1945	Lorraine
Foster	Sam	A	Jan 16,1945	
Maile	Edward F.	Sv		
Marble	Henry L.	A		
Parker	William F.	A		
Starr	Richard B.	Hq	May 3,1945	Lorraine
Turner	William K.	Sv	Jul 14,1945	Lorraine
Varrone	Peter	A	Dec 15,1944	Lorraine

494th Armored Field Artillery Battalion

Last Name	First Name	Co	Died	Buried
Bishop	Ernest	C	Jan 23,1945	Epinal
Bissmeyer	Roger G.	Hq		
Cauley	Calvin M.	A	Jan 22,1945	Epinal
Drescher	Robert W.	B	Jan 8,1945	Lorraine
Hart, Jr	Matthew P.	B		
Lamuth	Emil J.	Hq		
Lookabill	Benjamin F.	Hq		
Luizzi	Donato C.	A		
Maher	Thomas			
San Filippo	Raymond	C		
Urban	Henry S.	B	Dec 18,1944	Lorraine
Vasquez	Raoul F.	Hq		
Wilks	Homer D.	A	Apr 26,1945	Lorraine

495th Armored Field Artillery Battalion

Last Name	First Name	Co	Died	Buried
Finn	Joseph J.	Hq		
Handcock	Charles F.	Hq		
Karnash	John S.	Hq		
Klatt	Leonard	C	May 3,1945	Lorraine
Lindley	George E.	Hq		
Malmrose	Victor A.	B		
Pulley	Maurice W.	Hq		
Purvis, Jr	Warner S.	A		
Schwartz	Robert	C	May 3,1945	Lorraine
Wilson	Robert G.	B	Mar 21,1945	b

572nd Anti-Aircraft Artillery Battalion

Last Name	First Name	Co	Died	Buried
Carrol	Thomas			
Eves	Carl L.			
Flowers	Henry			
Hill	Obie D.			

Last Name	First Name	Co	Died	Buried
Hornbeck	Norman F.			
Kurowski	Clarence J.			
Myers	Stanley E			
Schoenke	Charles			
Seiffert	Joseph			
Suppa	Alphonso			

714th Tank Battalion

Last Name	First Name	Co	Died	Buried
Barnes	Hubert E.		Mar 22,1945	Lorraine
Blackard	Ferrel N.		Dec 15,1944	Lorraine
Blackburn, Jr.	John E.	B	Mar 22,1945	Lorraine
Blackham	Robert E.			
Blessing	Edwin L.	B	Mar 29,1945	Lorraine
Cook	George C.			
Cooke	Donald R.	B	Dec 23,1944	Lorraine
Davidson	Leroy J.	B		
Dodge	Fred E.	B	Mar 20,1945	
Downes	Amos A.		Dec 24,1944	Lorraine
Godwin	Erwin			
Gray	George P.		Apr 15,1945	Lorraine
Grillo, Jr.	Eugene			
Guld	Joseph B.			
Gurtz	William D.	B	Mar 29,1945	
Hake, Jr.	Charles	A	Apr 25,1945	Lorraine
Harman	Arnel S.	A		
Johnson	Noble K.		Dec 25,1944	Lorraine
Johnson	Thomas F.		Jan 14,1945	Epinal
Kacyon	Robert L.			
Kenyon	Robert L.	B	Mar 20,1945	
Kulpinski	Stanley	B	Mar 20,1945	Luxembourg
Lehmann	John J.			
Malleis	Erwin	SV		
Meiring	Richard F.	B	Jan 9,1945	Epinal
Osborne	Hobert	B	Mar 20,1945	Luxembourg
Panzino	Michael J.			
Parish	James M.	B	Mar 30,1945	
Peterson	Howard C.		Dec 23,1944	Lorraine
Pittman	Jesse J.	B	Jan 10,1945	
Poole	Thomas A.			
Roberts	Gordon R.	B	Jan 9,1945	Epinal
Rocky	Michael			

Last Name	First Name	Co	Died	Buried
Sachs	Robert K.	D	Jan 10,1945	Epinal
Sams	Thomas H.	B	Mar 20,1945	
Smith	Royce E.	B	Mar 20,1945	
Snow	Walter L.		Jan 10,1945	Epinal
Tankesley	Elmer F.	B	Jan 9,1945	
Tsimbidis	C.J.			
Warren	Manley M.	B	Mar 22,1945	Lorraine
White	Irvin M.		Dec 15,1944	Lorraine
Williams	Edward C.	B	Dec 23,1944	Lorraine

Headquarters

Last Name	First Name	Co	Died	Buried
Allison	Frederick J.	Band	Dec 17,1944	
Dowling	John W.	CCA	May 3,1945	
Zumbroich, Jr.	Herman	CCA	Apr 8,1945	
Walters	Edwin H.	CCB		

Total lives lost, all units—870

APPENDIX C

Army Organization

Below is a general description of the organizational structure of an Army unit, from the smallest organized unit to the largest. The numbers are not exact, but are a representation, and will give the reader a basic understanding of the table of organization of the United States Army.

Squad 10 men commanded by a sergeant

Platoon 36 men commanded by a lieutenant

Company 100 or more men commanded by a captain. Example: Company A, B, C, etc.
The artillery equivalent of a company is a battery, and the cavalry equivalent is a troop.

Battalion 1,000 men commanded by a lieutenant colonel

Combat Command 3,000 men commanded by a brigadier general

Division 11,000 men commanded by a major general

Corps Two or more divisions, commanded by a major general

Field Army Two or more corps, commanded by a lieutenant general

Army Group Two or more field armies, commanded by a lieutenant general or general

APPENDIX D

Overseas Wartime Assignments

Ninth Army	November 13, 1944
XV Corps	December 5, 1944
XXI Corps	December 27, 1944
Seventh Army	December 30, 1944
XV Corps	January 3, 1945
VI Corps	January 6, 1945
Seventh Army	January 21, 1945
First French Army	January 22, 1945
II French Corps	January 23, 1945
XXI Corps	February 3, 1945
Seventh Army	February 11, 1945
XV Corps	February 11, 1945
XXI Corps	February 28 1945
Third Army	March 17, 1945
XX Corps	March 17 1945
Seventh Army	March 24, 1945
XXI Corps	March 24, 1945
XV Corps	March 26, 1945
XXI Corps	March 31, 1945
Seventh Army	May 4, 1945

ENDNOTES

[1] Mark Skinner Watson, *Chief of Staff: Prewar Plans and Preparations* (Washington: Historical Division, Department of the Army, 1950), 16, 29, 155; Meirion and Susie Harries, *Soldiers of the Sun: The Rise and Fall of the Imperial Japanese Army* (New York: Random House, 1991), 318; Matthew Cooper, *The German Army: 1933-1945: Its Political and Military Failure* (New York: Bonanza Books, 1984), 164-165, 212; Martin van Creveld, *Fighting Power: German and U. S. Army Performance, 1939-1945* (Westport, Connecticut: Greenwood Press, 1982), 66.

[2] Kent Roberts Greenfield, Robert R. Palmer, and Bell I. Wiley, *The Army Ground Forces: The Organization of Ground Combat Troops* (Washington: Historical Division, Department of the Army, 1947), 9, 199, 252.

[3] Ibid., 189.

[4] Ibid., 161.

[5] Greenfield, 9; Robert R. Palmer, Bell I. Wiley, and William R. Keast, *The Army Ground Forces: The Procurement and Training of Ground Combat Troops*. (Washington, D.C.: Historical Division, Department of the Army, 1948), 161.

[6] Greenfield, 73.

[7] Shelby L. Stanton, *World War II Order of Battle* (New York: Galahad Books, 1984), 17.

[8] Palmer, 433-34.

[9] *A History of the United States Twelfth Armored Division: 15 September, 1942—17 December, 1945* (Baton Rouge: Army and Navy Publishing Company, 1947), 18; hereafter abbreviated *History*.

[10] Palmer, 433-436; *History*, 16.

[11] Stanton, 73.

[12] Bob Grebl, interview by author, 19 February 2004, Abilene, Texas. Mr. Grebl was a corporal in the 2nd Cavalry Division before going first to the 8th Armored Division, then to the 12th Armored Division, where he was an infantry squad leader.

[13] Ken Bradstreet, *The Hellcats: 12th Armored Division Association* (Paducah, Kentucky: Turner Publishing Company, 1987), 22; Palmer, 436-438.

[14] Bradstreet, 22.

[15] *History*, 17; Greenfield, 323.

[16] Bradstreet, 22.

[17] Greenfield, 323.

[18] *History*, 16; Palmer, 444.

[19] Palmer, 444-45; Bradstreet, 23.

[20] Palmer, 445-48.

[21] Bradstreet, 23.

[22] Bradstreet, 23.

[23] Grebl interview; *History*, 18.

[24] "Division C-G Praises Men For Fine Job," *Hellcat News*, 24 September 1943.

[25] *Hellcat News*, 15 October 1943, 5 November 1943.

[26] *Hellcat News*, 5 November 1943.

[27] Tracy M. Shilcutt, David Coffey and Donald S. Frazier, *Historic Abilene: An Illustrated History* (San Antonio: Historic Publishing Network, 2000), 11-14.

[28] Ibid., 23, 32.

[29] *Texas Almanac, 1941-42* (Dallas: A. H. Belo Corporation, 1941), 99, 509.

[30] Ty Cashion, *A Texas Frontier: The Clear Fork Country and Fort Griffin, 1849-1887* (Norman: University of Oklahoma Press, 1996), 25-26.

[31] Shilcutt, 38; White, Lonnie J. White, *Panthers to Arrowheads: The 36th (Texas-Oklahoma) Division in World War I* (Austin, Presidial Press, 1984). 20-25, 150-167.

[32] James M. Myers, "World War II as an Instrument of Social Modernization: The Social and Economic Influence of Camp Barkeley on Abilene, Texas." (Master's thesis, Hardin-Simmons University, Abilene, 1981), 5-8.

[33] Harry W. Dobbyn, *It Was Worth It! World War II With the Thunderbird Division* (Tampa, Florida: Free Press Publishing, 1976), 13-14; Myers, 10-12.

[34] Myers, 19; Dobbyn, 14-15.

[35] Dobbyn, 14-15.

[36] Myers, 20-21.

[37] "Mother Receives Honors For Dead Son," *U.S. Army Speedometer: Monthly Military Motor Magazine*, Volume 21 Number 5, May 1941 5, 10; "Laredo's only Medal of Honor winner remembered," *Laredo Morning Times*, 9 November 2002.

[38] Myers, 21-22.

[39] Stanton, 133-34.

[40] Bill Mauldin, *The Brass Ring* (New York: W. W. Norton & Company, 1971), iii, 60-62. 101, 113.

[41] Myers, 38-39

[42] George Wythe, *A History of the 90th Division* (The De Vinne Press, 1920), 3-7, 195-96.

[43] Mr. Robert Tiffany, interview by author, 15 March 2004, Abilene, Texas; Stanton, 163-64.

[44] *Abilene Reporter News*, 1 November 1943; Stanton, 63.

[45] Shilcutt, 48-51.

[46] Greenfield, 326.

[47] Greenfield, 327.

[48] Stanton, 17-19; Greenfield, 328.

[49] *History*, 19.

[50] Greenfield, 320-21.

[51] "12th Armored Division Commander at Barkeley," *Abilene Reporter News*, November 17, 1943; "12th Armored 'Hellcats' Are at Barkeley," Ibid., November 21, 1943.

[52] Andrew Jack Winter, Personal Memoir, Archives, 12th Armored Division Memorial Museum, Abilene, Texas.

[53] Stanton, 299.

[54] "714th Tk Bn Returns To 12th Family Fold," *Hellcat News*, 2 March 1944.

[55] "'Grasshopper Patrol' Important Element Of Division In Combat," *Hellcat News*, 2 March 1944.

[56] "Division's Harvester Battalion Has Unique History In Army," *Hellcat News*, 2 March 1944.

[57] "USO Offers Concert For Devotees Of 'Long Hair',"*Hellcat News*, 16 March 1944.

[58] Bradstreet, vol.1, 41; "Hellcat Holiday Proclaimed Hit By GI Audiences," *Hellcat News*, 20 April 1944.

[59] "Hubert Taylor Snares Top Honors In Rodeo," *Hellcat News*, 8 June 1944.

[60] "General Brewer Welcomes ASTP Men To 12th Division," *Hellcat News*, 30 March 1944.

[61] *History*, 22; Bradstreet, vol. 1, 35.

[62] "12th Armored Division Commander At Barkeley," *Abilene Reporter News*, 17 November 1943; Bradstreet, Vol. 1, 11, 192

[63] *History*, 22; "The General's Message," *Hellcat News*, 22 June 1944; Ibid., 29 June 1944; Ibid., 20 July 1944..

[64] F. George Hatt, Jr., *17th Armored Infantry Battalion Historical Information (Updated)* (Abilene: Abilene Christian University History Department, 1998), 5-6; Hereafter Hatt *17th AIB*; F. George Hatt, Jr., "The 12th Armored Division at Camp Barkeley, Texas and Overseas," *Armored Men* 2 (Fall 1998): 50-51; Carl J. Lyons, "World War II Experiences of Carl J. Lyons: Company A, 17th Armored Infantry Battalion, 12th Armored Division, United States Army" Personal memoir, Archives, 12th Armored Division Memorial Museum, Abilene, Texas, 6.

[65] Bradstreet, vol.1, 54; Carold W. Bland, "Quickly Passes The Time Of Dreams," Manuscript, December 1994, Archives, 12th Armored Division Memorial Museum, Abilene, Texas, 66.

[66] Hatt, *17th AIB*, 6-7; *History*, 23; Marvin Tishcoff, "A Hellcat Abroad," personal memoir, 1992, 9..

[67] Simon Kops, "The Other Little Corporal: A Worm's Eye View of the War," Personal memoir, Archives, 12th Armored Division Memorial Museum, 32-33.

[68] Stephen Czecha, Personal memoir, Archives, 12th Armored Division Memorial Museum.

[69] Hatt, *17th AIB*, 6-7.

[70] Bradstreet, Vol. 1, 55.

[71] Roderick Allen File, Archives, 12th Armored Division Memorial Museum, Abilene, Texas.

[72] *History*, 24; Lyons 9.

[73] Czecha memoir.

[74] Bland, 66-67; Kops, 37.

[75] *History*, 24; Tishcoff, 13-14.

[76] *History*, 24-25.

[77] *Combat Highlights of the United States Twelfth Armored Division in the European Theater of Operations, 1 December 1944-30 May 1945*, (G-3 Information and Education Section, 1945), 4; hereafter *Combat Highlights*.

[78] *Combat Highlights*, 4-5; *History*, 27.

[79] Lyons, 12-13.

[80] *Combat Highlights*, 5; Hatt, *17th AIB*, 8-9.

[81] Hatt, *17th AIB*, 9.

[82] Bradstreet, Volume II, 28; *Combat Highlights*, 6.

[83] *History*, 28-30.

[84] Charles Whiting, *The Other Battle of the Bulge: Operation Northwind* (Chelsea, Michigan: Scarborough House, 1986), 11, 18.

[85] *The Initial Assault on Herrlisheim by CCB, 12th Armored Division* by Committee 7, Officers Advanced Course (Fort Knox, Kentucky: The Armored School, 1950), 1,2; Jeffrey J. Clarke and Robert Ross Smith, *Riviera to the Rhine* (Washington, D.C.: Center of Military History, United States Army, 1991), 514-15.

[86] Hatt, *17th AIB*, 10-12.

[87] *Initial Assault on Herrlisheim*, 4-20.

[88] Hatt, *17th AIB*, 10,12.

[89] Clarke, 523-24.

90 Czecha memoir, written October 1, 2001.

91 Hatt, *17th AIB*, 12-14; *43rd Tank Battalion Unit History*, (Wurttenberg, Germany, Schwabenverlag Printing Office, 1945), 17.

92 Clarke, 524-25; *43rd Tank Battalion Unit History*, 18-19.

93 Hatt, *17th AIB*, 15-17.

94 *Combat Highlights*, 16-18.

95 *Combat Highlights*, 18.

96 Clarke, 533-41.

97 *History*, 49-53; Clarke, 550-51.

98 *Combat Highlights*, 25.

99 Clarke, 553-55.

100 *History*, 53-54; *Combat Highlights*, 25-26.

101 *Combat Highlights*, 29; *History*, 54-56.

102 *Combat Highlights*, 29; Allene G. Carter, *Honoring Sergeant Carter: Redeeming a Black World War II Hero's Legacy* (New York: Harper Collins, 2003), 20, 29; Ulysses Lee, *The Employment of Negro Troops* (Washington, D.C.: Center of Military History, United States Army, 1966), 699-700.

103 *History*, 54-55; *Combat Highlights*, 29.

104 *Combat Highlights*, 29-31; History, 55-56.

105 *Combat Highlights*, 31-34.

106 *History*, 62.

107 *Combat Highlights*, 33-34.

108 *Forty-third Tank Battalion Unit History*, (Ellwangen, Germany: Schwabenverlag Printing Office, 1945), 30-31.

109 *History*, 66-70.

110 *Combat Highlights*, 36-37.

111 Ibid., 37-38.

112 Julien D. Saks, Personal Memoir, Archives, 12th Armored Division Memorial Museum, Abilene, Texas.

113 Ibid., 33, 38-39.

114 *History*, 72-78; *Combat Highlights*, 38-42.

115 *History*, 78-79.

116 Vertical files, Archives, 12th Armored Division Memorial Museum, Abilene, Texas.

117 *History*, 86-87.

BIBLIOGRAPHY

Books

Mauldin, Bill. *The Brass Ring: A Sort of a Memoir.* New York: W. W. Norton & Company, 1971.

Bradstreet, Ken. *Hellcats: 12th Armored Division Association, Volume I.* Paducah, Kentucky: Turner Publishing Company, 1987.

Bradstreet, Ken. Hellcats: *12th Armored Division Association, Volume II.* Paducah, Kentucky: Turner Publishing Company, 1990.

Cashion, Ty. *A Texas Frontier: The Clear Fork Country and Fort Griffin, 1849-1887.* Norman: University of Oklahoma Press, 1996.

Clarke, Jeffrey J. and Robert Ross Smith. *Riviera to the Rhine.* Washington, D.C.: Center of Military History, United States Army, 1991.

Cooper, Matthew. *The German Army: 1933-1945: Its Political and Military Failure.* New York: Bonanza Books, 1984.

Dobbyn, Harry W. *It Was Worth It! World War II With the Thunderbird Division.* Tampa, Florida: Free Press Publishing, 1976.

Greenfield, Kent Roberts, Robert R. Palmer, and Bell I. Wiley. *The Army Ground Forces: The Organization of Ground Combat Troops.* Washington, D.C.: Historical Division, Department of the Army, 1947.

Harries, Meirion and Susie. *Soldiers of the Sun: The Rise and Fall of the Imperial Japanese Army.* New York: Random House, 1991.

Hatt, Fenwick George. *17th Armored Infantry Battalion Historical Information (Updated).* Abilene, Texas: Abilene Christian University History Department, 1998.

Lee, Ulysses. *The Employment of Negro Troops.* Washington, D.C.: Center of Military History, United States Army, 1966.

Palmer, Robert R., Bell I. Wiley, and William R. Keast. *The Army Ground Forces: The Procurement and Training of Ground Combat Troops.* Washington, D.C.: Historical Division, Department of the Army, 1948.

Shilcutt, Tracy M., David Coffey, and Donald S. Frazier. *Historic Abilene: An Illustrated History.* San Antonio: Historical Publishing Network, 2000.

Stanton, Shelby L. *World War II Order of Battle.* New York: Galahad Books, 1984.

van Creveld, Martin. *Fighting Power: German and U. S. Army Performance, 1939-1945.* Westport, Connecticut: Greenwood Press, 1982.

Watson, Mark Skinner. *Chief of Staff: Prewar Plans and Preparations.* Washington, D.C. Historical Division, Department of the Army, 1950.

White, Lonnie J. *Panthers to Arrowheads: The 36th (Texas-Oklahoma) Division in World War I.* Austin: Presidial Press, 1984.

Wythe, George. *A History of the 90th Division.*: The De Vinne Press, 1920.

Texas Almanac: 1941-42. Dallas: A. H. Belo Corporation, 1941.

The Hellcats in World War II: A History of the United States Twelfth Armored Division: 15 September, 1942—17 December, 1945. Baton Rouge: Army and Navy Publishing Company, 1947.

Forty-third Tank Battalion Unit History From Dec. 7, 1944 to May 9, 1945. Ellwangen, Germany: Schwabenverlag Printing Office, 1945.

Interviews

Grebl, Robert. Interview by author. 19 February 2004, Abilene, Texas.

Tiffany, Robert. Interview by author. 15 March 2004, Abilene, Texas.

Magazines

U.S. Army Speedometer: Monthly Military Motor Magazine. May 1941.

Newspapers

Abilene Reporter News. 17 November 1943.

Hellcat News. 24 September 1943.

Laredo Morning Times. 9 November 2002.

Theses

Myers, James M. "World War II As An Instrument of Social Modernization: The Social and Economic Influence of Camp Barkeley on Abilene, Texas." Master's thesis, Hardin-Simmons University, Abilene, 1981.

Memoirs

Bland, Carold. "Quickly Passes the Time of Dreams," Personal Memoir. Archives, 12th Armored Division Memorial Museum, Abilene, Texas.

Czecha, Stephen. Personal Memoir. 1 October 2001. Archives, 12th Armored Division Memorial Museum, Abilene, Texas.

Lyons, Carl J. "World War II Experiences of Carl J. Lyons: Company A, 17th Armored Infantry

Battalion, 12th Armored Division, United States Army." Personal Memoir. Archives, 12th Armored Division Memorial Museum, Abilene, Texas.

Winter, Andrew Jack. Personal Memoir. Archives, 12th Armored Division Memorial Museum, Abilene, Texas.

Journals

Hatt, Fenwick George, Jr. "The 12th Armored Division at Camp Barkeley, Texas and overseas." *Armored Men* 2 (Fall 1998): 45-57.

INDEX